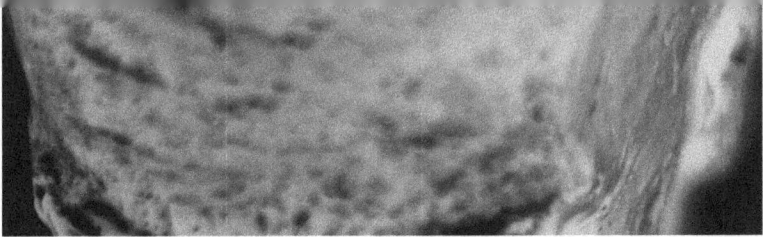

Durkheim Today

Durkheim Today

Edited by *W. S. F. Pickering*

Introduction by Kenneth Thompson

Berghahn Books
New York • Oxford

Published in association with the British Centre for Durkheimian Studies

First published in 2002 by **Berghahn Books**
www.BerghahnBooks.com

©2002 Durkheim Press

Library of Congress Cataloging-in-Publication Data
Durkheim today / edited by W.S.F. Pickering : introduction by
Kenneth Thompson.
    p, cm.
Includes bibliographical references and index.
ISBN 1-57181-548-1 (cloth : alk. paper)
    1. Sociology--Philosophy. 2. Durkheim, Emile. 1858-1917--
Contributions in sociology.
1. Pickering. W.S.F.

HM585 .D87 2002
301.01--dc21
                                                            2002018432

British Library Cataloguing in Publication Data
A catalogue record for this book is available from the British Library
Printed in the United States on acid-free paper
ISBN 1-57181-548-1 hardback

Contents

Contributors

Philippe Besnard was born in 1942. He is director of research at the Centre National de la Recherche Scientifique in Paris and teaches at the Institut d'Etudes Politiques. He is joint-editor of the *Revue française de sociologie*. For many years he was an active member of the Groupe d'études durkheimiennes, an international network he created. Among the several books he has published are *The Sociological Domain* (1983) and *L'Anomie* (1987).

Mike Gane is Professor in the Department of Social Sciences at Loughborough University. He has written *On Durkheim's Rules of Sociological Method* (1988) and edited *The Radical Sociology of Durkheim and Mauss* (1992). He has also recently edited a book of interviews with Jean Baudrillard and written a book on theory, theorists and gender, both published by Routledge in 1993.

Josep R. Llobera is a retired Senior Lecturer in Sociology and Social Anthropology at Goldsmiths' College and Honorary Professor in University College, University of London. He has published extensively on the history of the social sciences and on nationalism. His latest book is *The Development of Nationalism in Western Europe* (1994).

W. S. F. Pickering is a retired lecturer in sociology from the University of Newcastle upon Tyne. In 1991 he helped to found the British Centre for Durkheimian Studies in the Institute of Social and Cultural Anthropology, Oxford, of which he is General Secretary. He has written and edited books on Durkheim and published articles on him and members of the Année Sociologique group.

Warren Schmaus is the author of *Durkheim's Philosophy of Science and the Sociology of Knowledge* (1994), as well as numerous articles in the history and philosophy of the social sciences and on issues of science and values. He is Professor of Philosophy at the Illinois Institute of Technology in Chicago and a fellow of the Center of the Philosophy of Science at the University of Pittsburgh.

Sue Stedman Jones studied philosophy and completed a London doctorate titled 'From Kant to Durkheim'. She formerly taught social philosophy and the philosophy of the social sciences at Goldsmith's College, University of London. She is now pursuing independent research and has just completed a book, *Durkheim Reconsidered*. She divides her time between London and Paris.

Philippe Steiner teaches economics and sociology and is Professor in the University of Lille. His published works include *La Sociologie de Durkheim*; (with J.-J. Gislain) *La Sociologie économique (1890-1920)*; *Essai sur la rationalisation de la connaissance économique*. He is a member of the management board of the *Revue française de sociologie*.

Geoffrey Walford is Professor in Education Policy and a Fellow of Green College at the University of Oxford. He was previously Senior Lecturer in Sociology and Education Policy at Aston Business School, Aston University, Birmingham. He has written extensively on various aspects of educational practice and policy.

Willie Watts Miller is editor of *Durkheim Studies/Etudes durkheimiennes*. His publications include *Durkheim, Morals and Modernity* (1996) and a critical edition and translation of Durkheim's Latin thesis on Montesquieu. He is Senior Lecturer in the Department of Sociology in the University of Bristol.

Preface

What are scholars who write on Durkheim today saying about this founding father of sociology? This small book sets out to answer the question in a succinct way and at the same time to show the stage which Durkheimian studies have now reached. Its brevity bars it from being considered in any way an exhaustive or definitive study. Nevertheless, it does point its readers to the paths scholars are now following as they examine the various themes of study which Durkheim opened up to the academic world.

The book has another merit in so far as at the present time a large number of books and articles are appearing on Durkheim, some in obscure places. The non-professional reader may care to know why and how scholars select from the mass of material available what they consider the most important contributions to Durkheimian scholarship. Such a selection forms the basis of this book.

Growth in the interest in Durkheim began in the 1970s and continues to grow (see Chapter 2). Part of such blossoming has come with the creation in 1991 of the British Centre for Durkheimian Studies which was founded in Oxford under the aegis of the Institute of Social and Cultural Anthropology. Amongst other things it publishes its own books and an annual periodical.

Late in 2000, in conjunction with the Centre, Routledge published a four-volume collection of articles and chapters of books, nearly all of which had appeared since 1990, called in short, *Durkheim. Critical Assessments.** Emerging from these volumes, too expensive for most individuals to buy, has come this book. It should be noted that two earlier sets of critical assessments had aleady appeared.

This last set of volumes was divided into various areas covered by Durkheim's thought, such as method, religion, politics, morals, education and so forth. The areas chosen very largely but not entirely followed the divisions set out by Durkheim himself in his famous journal, *L'Année sociologique*. Eight specialists in these areas were asked to select for reproduction about a dozen articles or chapters of books which they thought were the most relevant to their area. Preceding the reproduction of the items in each section, the specialist was asked to write a short introduction, referring to the items he had chosen and also 'giving the state of play' in that particular field.

This book is based on such introductions. Some, however, have been slightly altered from what originally appeared in the *Critical Assessments*. One reason for the changes is that the book needed a slightly different presentation from that in the parent volumes. In one or two cases, experts wanted to bring yet further up-to-date what they had originally written. The items chosen for reproduction, however, have in no way been changed. One chapter does not contain any such items and stands on its own. It is the final chapter which was an overall introduction to the parent volumes. It is written as a critical review of the way the works of Durkheim have been generally interpreted over past years and suggests new ways of moving forwards.

*W. S. F. Pickering (ed.) 2001 *Emile Durkheim. Critical Assessments of Leading Sociologists*, Third Series, London and New York: Routledge, Taylor and Francis.

Referencing

Where in the various chapters, there are references in round brackets ( ), they refer to a book or article which is located in the references immediately following the text itself. Square brackets [ ] in the text usually but not always contain simply a name which refers to the author of an item that has been chosen for reproduction in the relevant section of *Emile Durkheim Critical Assessments*, Third Series. Details of the items are found under Selected Items, which follow after the References of the chapter. If there are two or more reproductions by the same author in the one chapter, the relevant dates are included with the name in order to distinguish them.

References to works by Durkheim are in most cases according to the dating-enumeration of that established by Steven Lukes in his *Emile Durkheim. His Life and Work: A Historical and Critical Study* (1973, Allen Lane, London; 1992, reprinted with the bibliography updated, Penguin, London).

Acknowledgements

The Editor wishes to thank Routledge, Taylor and Francis for their permission and encouragement to reproduce the Introductions in the Third Series of *Emile Durkheim. Critical Assessments of Leading Sociologists.* He would like to express a warm word of gratitude to those members of staff who so patiently helped him in the production of the four volumes, especially Frances Parkes and Natalie Foster.

The whole project, along with this book, would never have seen the light of day without the unstinting hard work and co-operation of his colleagues who were responsible for the various sections and to others who offered advice and guidance.

Finally, a word of sincere appreciation to Kirsty McCormack, who did much to prepare this book.

Introduction

Kenneth Thompson

In order to build on the foundations laid by Durkheim it is first necessary to gain an accurate appreciation of his works and those of his collaborators. Such has been the principal aim of the British Centre for Durkheimian Studies, as exemplified in this volume. Through their research, conferences and publications, scholars associated with the Centre have considerably advanced understanding of Durkheimian sociology. One of the guiding principles in the execution of their task has been to place Durkheim's thought in the social and intellectual context of his time. In some cases this has meant elucidating the philosophical roots of his thought and tracing their relationship to those of other significant figures. A good example is Susan Stedman Jones's exposure of the philosophical debt that Durkheim owed to Renouvier when developing his case for treating social facts as 'things'. She shows that a proper understanding of this philosophical context would have rendered implausible the frequently heard accusation that Durkheim was a crude positivist.

The same kind of detailed scrutiny has been applied to disentangling the eclectic and polemical aspects of his works – aspects that may account for the diverse and often contradictory labels that have been attached to his positions in the past. For example, Warren Schmaus, in his discussion here of Durkheim's epistemology and philosophy of science, suggests why the eclectic character of *The Rules of Sociological Method* (1895a) may have led to him being described variously as a rationalist, a realist, and even an essentialist. Frequently, too, Durkheim was engaged in a polemic that led him to construct his arguments around sets of dichotomies, which can appear to lead him into extreme and apparently dogmatic statements, such as seemingly emphasising social determinism at the expense of individual will. Stedman Jones's 'Reflections on the interpretation of Durkheim in the sociological tradition' should finally lay to rest some of the main misrepresentations.

This stripping away of many of the misconceptions that have arisen about Durkheim's sociology over the years is a welcome step forward. There are also positive indications of where Durkheimian scholarship may lead us in the future, especially in re-examining neglected aspects such as his contribution towards the development of a sociology of the social and moral embeddedness of economic behaviour (Philippe Steiner's chapter) and with regard to developing a theory of social bonding that encompasses the two dimensions of integration and regulation (Philippe Besnard's discussion, 'Suicide and anomie'). This is surely: 'Durkheim today and for tomorrow'.

We know that every so often in the history of sociology there is a 'return to the classics' with the aim of finding there new inspiration and justification for a theoretical shift in the discipline (as Mike Gane makes clear in Chapter 2). Almost more than any other major theorist, Durkheim has been found useful for achieving this purpose. Perhaps it is due to the breadth and variety of his works, or to their capacity to be read in different ways. Whatever the reason, there can be no denying the fact that re-reading Durkheim has been the prelude to a number of theoretical developments in the history of sociology, which is also richly illustrated by the contents of this book.

Some commentators have simply paid their respects to Durkheim's pioneering efforts and then moved on to criticise his shortcomings as a way of preparing the ground for their own, supposedly superior, formulations. For others, however, their re-reading is a voyage of discovery or re-discovery in the course of which Durkheim's ideas yield new insights and useful conceptual resources. This has been the case with the so-called 'cultural turn' that has had a substantial impact on sociology in recent years, especially in North America. The other 'founding fathers' of sociology did not provide anything to compare with the extensive programme for cultural analysis that is found in Durkheim's turn towards a sustained focus on cultural analysis in his later works, especially in *The Elementary Forms of Religious Life* (some of the broader relevance of this work, beyond the narrow boundaries of the sociology of religion, is suggested by Pickering in Chapter 3). Theorists in the Marxian tradition have undoubtedly made contributions to cultural studies, but Marx's own works contain only the vaguest suggestions for a sociological theory of modern culture. While Weber's *verstehen* methodology certainly helped to advance hermeneutic analysis, his own theses of the 'loss of meaning' and the substitution of formal rationality for substantive value rationality in modern society left little scope for a theory of culture. By contrast, Durkheim provides useful tools for investigating symbolic structures and processes in the modern world. His insights into the significance in all societies of binary categories, such as the sacred versus the profane, the pure and the polluted, the 'we' and the 'other', have promoted not only the structuralist method of analysis, but also a renewed appreciation of the relative autonomy and causal significance of cultural logics. In other words, contrary to the tendency of some other schools of sociology, the Durkheimian school does not subordinate culture to social structural factors. Although symbolic systems originally bear the marks of the social structures in which they originated, once formed they become relatively autonomous and become causal factors in their own right. As Robert Bellah puts it: 'While collective representations (which Durkheim later calls "ideals" and which we might call "values") ... arise from and reflect the "social substratum" (the morphological variables), they are, once in existence, "partially autonomous realities" which independently influence subsequent social development' (Bellah 1959:457).

It is not only the cultural analysis in *The Elementary Forms of the Religious Life* (1912a) that has provided new sources of inspiration for recent developments in sociology. Other works that have attracted renewed attention, even after initially having been neglected, are *Professional Ethics and Civic Morals* (1957a) and *The Evolution of Educational Thought* (1938a). The former has proved particularly relevant to debates about 'civil society' (see Llobera's contribution to this volume), while the latter has contributed to the study of cultural and institutional change by distinguishing between the production and selection of new educational ideologies, on the one hand, and their institutionalization, on the other (the relevance of this work to contemporary educational issues is suggested in Walford's chapter).

Much of political sociology involving historical-comparative analysis, from the 1960s onwards, tended to revolve around the concepts of the modern state and capitalist social relations (classes). The main sources of inspiration were Weber and Marx. Little attention was given to the associational relations of civil life. It is only since the revival of interest in the concept of civil society, after the fall of the Communist regimes in 1989 and the beginning of efforts to rebuild the institutions of civil society there, that fresh attention has been given to Durkheim's political sociology. Durkheim's studies of the intermediate domains of society and their contribution to social integration, individual autonomy and willed community, anticipated precisely those elements featured in contemporary analyses of civil society - the differentiated 'structures of socialization, association, and organized forms of communication of the lifeworld to the extent that these are institutionalized or are in the process of being institutionalized' (Cohen and Arato 1992:x). Durkheim's political sociology, which was once regarded as almost non-existent, or of little contemporary relevance, is now appreciated as offering a 'communication theory of politics that seems quite contemporary' (Bellah 1973:xxxiv). He distinguishes between the administrative, coercive, and intelligence functions of political and state institutions. The discussion, in *Professional Ethics and Civic Morals*, of the state's intelligence functions, which are concerned with the formulation of collective representations distinguished by their higher degree of consciousness and reflection, and so distilling and elevating the ideals and beliefs of the prereflective masses, has proved particularly fertile. His analysis resembles what Habermas and others have termed the 'public sphere of civil society'.

It is also in relation to analyses of the narratives and discourses that appear in the public sphere of civil society that Durkheim's ideas about binary codes have been found most useful. The American sociologist, Jeffrey Alexander, has been prominent in promoting this type of Durkheimian cultural sociology. He demonstrates its usefulness in deconstructing such narratives into binary sets of good and evil characteristics, as in his case study of the Watergate crisis and its unfolding as a public drama of ritual cleansing (Alexander 1988). Another fruitful Durkheimian concept in this context is that of moments or episodes of 'collective effervescence'. Durkheim used examples ranging from primitive religion to the French Revolution to illustrate these potentially creative and dynamic moments. They served not just to reproduce the society through the experience of a heightened sense of collective identity, but also (in certain situations) to transform social relations: 'There are periods in history when, under the influence of some great collective shock, social interactions have become more frequent and active. Men look for each other and assemble together more than ever. That general effervescence results which is characteristic of revolutionary or creative epochs' (Durkheim 1912a/t, 1915d: 210–1). Alexander develops this idea to show how, in episodes of collective effervescence, the classificatory systems of collective symbols can sometimes be drastically changed or adapted. 'Cultural myths are recalled and extended to contemporary circumstances. Social solidarities are reworked' (Alexander 1988:192). This adaptation of Durkheim's ideas is not only fruitful for analyses of contemporary political episodes, such as the Watergate crisis, it also calls into question earlier criticisms of Durkheim for allegedly focusing solely on social reproduction and failing to offer a theory of social change other than the social evolutionary. It also serves to refute those critics who have suggested that Durkheim's sociologism was pursued at the expense of any consideration of social psychological factors in political and other spheres. One of his points about periods of collective effervescence was that they revealed the processes of heightened emotional intensity that bind groups and institutions together, especially through the attachments to sacred symbols and systems of classification. This perspective has proved particularly useful in the study of nationalism, revolutionary politics, and theories of new social movements, such as Maffesoli's *The Time of the Tribes* (referred to by W. Watts Miller in his contribution to this volume).

Another key figure, in the recent revival of a Durkheimian cultural sociology in America, is Robert Bellah. In the immediate post-war decades he was one of the most influential commentators on Durkheim's work, especially on the sociology of morals, and developed the concept of 'civil religion' to demonstrate the viability of the idea that every society has a religious dimension. However, it might be argued that his greatest contribution to the development of Durkheimian cultural sociology has been through the publication of the jointly-authored best-seller, *Habits of the Heart: Individualism and Commitment in America* (Bellah et al., 1985). This study of the tensions between the values of community and individualism in America under the impact of the pressures of neo-liberal individualism shows the continuing relevance of Durkheim's concerns. They are concerns that feature in W. Watts Miller's chapter on 'Morality and Ethics', where he also points out the relevance of Durkheim's ideas about moral education to the recent debates around Foucault's theory of 'governmentality' and forms of self-governance in liberal-democratic society. Of course, from a Durkheimian perspective, the workings of the disciplinary phenomena as described by Foucault would appear to be a pathological imbalance in the relations between individual and community. Nevertheless, it is intriguing that Foucault, like Durkheim, focused on the significance of the development of forms of moral regulation based on self-governance as character-istic of modern liberal-democratic society. To what extent Foucault was directly influenced by Durkheim's work is not clear. At the opposite end of the political spectrum to this Durkheimian-Foucaultian theme of self-surveillance and self-governance in liberal society there is the equally Durkheimian theme of the revival of the sacred and collective effervescence in the new social movements and 'affinity' – based groups as developed in Maffesoli's *The Time of the Tribes: The Decline of Individualism in Mass Society* (1996) and by Philip Mellor and Chris Shilling, *Re-forming the Body: Religion, Community and Modernity* (1997). In these works, the trend towards excessive individualism is considered to be intolerable to many people, who react by seeking a sacred bonding through commitment to movements or groups which offer ways of 'keeping warm together' against the cold winds of modernity and the alienating experience of the economic-political order. Of course, the emotional warmth of sacred bonds can also be generated by violence and deviance, whether it be in gangs or extreme political groups. The sacred and collective effervescence, as Durkheim made clear, is based on excess, and this can take many forms – an insight developed by Bataille, Callois and the College de Sociologie (discussed by Pickering in the following section on 'Religion'). Some of the scenes of violence involving anti-capitalist demonstrators protesting at meetings of the 'G8' world leaders in recent years, illustrate the relevance of this analysis.

These are just a few of the themes featured in the following sections of this book, but they serve to demonstrate the continuing importance of Durkheim's works and the benefits to be derived from re-reading them in the light of contemporary social developments. After all, Durkheim made it clear that, whilst his aim was to develop an academic discipline of sociology that would have the same intellectual rigour as any other, the choice of topics to be studied was not arbitrary. In his view, modern society fell far short of the Enlightenment vision of a rational and just social order - it suffered from a persistent malaise. At its best, Durkheimian sociology has always maintained that critical edge.

References

Alexander, J. C. 1988 'Culture and Political Crisis: "Watergate" and Durkheimian Sociology', pp. 187-224 in *Durkheimian Sociology: Cultural Studies*, edited by Jeffrey C. Alexander, Cambridge: Cambridge University Press.

Bellah, R. N. 1959 'Durkheim and History', *American Sociological Review* 24: 447-465.

Bellah, R. N. 1973 'Introduction', pp. Ix-Iv in *Emile Durkheim: On Morality and Society*, edited by Robert N. Bellah, Chicago: University of Chicago Press.

Bellah, R. N., Madsen, R., Sullivan, W. M., Swidler, A. and Tipton, S. M. 1985 *Habits of the Heart: Individualism and Commitment in American Life*, New York: Harper Row. Cohen, J. L. and Arato, A. 1992 *Civil Society and Political Theory*, Cambridge, Mass.: MIT Press.

Durkheim, E. [For the various books and other works by Durkheim and their translations into English, see S. Lukes, 1973/1992 *Emile Durkheim. His Life and Work: A Historical and Critical Study*, London: Penguin Books.]

Maffesoli, M. 1996 *The Time of the Tribes: The Decline of Individualism in Mass Society*, London: Sage.

Mellor, P. A. and Shilling, C. 1997 *Re-forming the Body: Religion, Community and Modernity*, London: Sage.

Chapter 1

Durkheim: the man himself and his heritage

W. S. F. Pickering

After Durkheim died in 1917 his disciples, particularly Marcel Mauss and Paul Fauconnet, set about making his academic work more widely known and hopefully, better appreciated. They did so by publishing some of his lectures, various manuscripts, and reproducing in book-form articles published earlier in journals, both popular and less well-known. One can point to six or more posthumous books whose publication further established Durkheim as the late nineteenth-century pioneer and grand master of French sociology (see references to these books and articles in Lukes 1973:586–90). But very little was or could be published about his life. The reason was simply the fact that only limited material has been bequeathed to posterity. As is common knowledge, letters, manuscripts and other materials disappeared during World War II. In 1943 the Nazis occupied his daughter's house in which all his manuscripts were kept and threw them, along with domestic items, onto the street. She had left before they arrived. Tragically, the house was then turned into a horrifying place of interrogation and torture. Thus, in comparison with other great writers and thinkers, there has been very limited material to be put into the hands of biographers, although little by little letters written by Durkheim are coming to light. One recent exception to the paucity of information has been the publication of letters Durkheim wrote to Marcel Mauss, his nephew (Durkheim 1998a. A selection is given here). It is not surprising therefore that scholars, who in the past and today try to understand both his domestic and

professional life, have tended to speculate about issues and problems that might never have arisen had more material been
available. One or two of these issues which have recently come
to the fore we now turn to.

It has often been the assumption amongst those who read
Durkheim that he quickly gained personal success in establishing sociology as an academic discipline in French universities.
Such is not the case [Karady]. He had to fight hard to obtain its
recognition in Faculties of Letters. Sociology became known
through his giving courses on education and presenting lectures
which were not part of a degree course. At least two factors
accounted for his eventual success – the need for some kind of
unifying ideology for the Third Republic against a very politically divided France, and in his gathering around him a group of
brilliant, young disciples, who were able to publish the highly
regarded journal, *L'Année sociologique* (see Preface). Competi-
tion within the universities about the curricula remained
strong and it was difficult to find a place for sociology. But
Durkheim faced other problems. He was disappointed about the
reception of his book on suicide published in 1897, which he
thought so important. In addition, *L'Année sociologique* was not
easy to produce and demanded a great amount of time. And he
was upset that he was not appointed to a professorship in Paris.
Only in 1902 did he receive a teaching post there. Until then
he was lecturer and then professor in Bordeaux [Durkheim's
Lettres].

After his death things became no easier for the Durkheimian
cause. Indeed, following World War I there was vigorous opposition to Durkheim's aim that social phenomena should be studied
through scientific analysis. The opposition was to some degree
precipitated by the enthusiasm of his own disciples in seeking a
prominent place for his work in readers (*manuels*) which
students were required to study in the Ecoles Normales (teachers' training colleges). The opposition won the day and a
government minister was forced to resign. It is probably true to
say that just before World War II, while certain beacons burned

to keep Durkheim's name alive, the esteem accorded to the Durkheimian school reached a nadir. Mauss, who automatically assumed Durkheim's role when he died, proved to be not the leader his uncle was. He had great difficulty in trying to hold together and above all expand the Année Sociologique group, which was decimated by those killed in the First World War. The journal, which had been so prominent, virtually fell by the wayside.

Revivals began to occur in the 1960s and 1970s. The first was due to the work of the anthropologist, Lévi-Strauss, who became very much the *philosophe* of his day and whose thought was strongly influenced by Durkheim (see Hamnett in Chapter 3). Another avenue of revival came from the work of the British scholar, Steven Lukes. His intellectual biography, originally written as a doctoral thesis, was published in 1973. The supervisor was an Oxford anthropologist, Professor E. E. Evans-Pritchard. It should be noted that a small band of anthropologists in Oxford, before and particularly after World War II, had been responsible for making Durkheim's work (together with that of his disciples) known more widely through their teaching and through initiating English translations of books written by Durkheimians. We refer to such scholars as Radcliffe-Brown, Evans-Pritchard, Rodney Needham and David Pocock. It should be noted in passing that Durkheim himself made no distinction between anthropology and sociology. At the same time some interest was shown by sociologists in Britain but they were not as enthusiastic as were the anthropologists and were mostly influenced by American interpretations of Durkheim (see Introduction here). One notable exception in recent times is Anthony Giddens, now Director of the London School of Economics.

The thoroughness of Lukes' book has made it an authoritative work which is not likely to be superceded in the forseeable future. Although some scholars would disagree with some of Lukes' interpretations of Durkheim's ideas, the fact remains that the book stands as a *vade-mecum* (Lukes 1973).

In the United States from the time of the First World War, the study of Durkheim rather than that of his disciples has had an honourable following. The first translation into English of any of his major works was undertaken in 1915 when J. W. Swain translated *Les Formes élémentaires de la vie religieuse*. It was published first in New York and then shortly afterwards in London. The Americans were involved in further translations – *The Division of Labour in Society* in 1933, *The Rules of Sociological Method* in 1938, *Suicide: a Study in Sociology* in 1951, *Education and Sociology* in 1952, *Socialism and Saint-Simon* in 1958, *Montesquieu and Rousseau* in 1960, *Moral Education* in 1961. These American translations have led the way in making Durkheim's works known around the English-speaking world. In the realm of interpretation, Talcott Parsons, writing in the late 1930s, gave Durkheim a prominent place in his quest for establishing a new genre of sociology in his once popular book, *The Structure of Social Action* (Parsons 1937; and see Chapter 10 here).

In the growth of Durkheimian studies – and we concentrate on those of Durkheim himself – scholars have specialized in particular areas of social phenomena by going beyond what Lukes and earlier scholars have written. In such a development, one field that has fascinated sociologists is methodology. This has attracted scholars such as J.-M. Berthelot, M. Gane and R. A. Jones. In the matter of Durkheim's approach to religion, K. Thompson, F.-A. Isambert and W. S. F. Pickering have written extensively on the subject. And in other areas D. Bloor, B. Barnes and W. Schmaus have concentrated on Durkheim's epistemology: on morality F.-A. Isambert and W. Watts Miller have made contributions, as has P. Besnard on suicide and anomie. And there have been those who have written in more general terms covering a number of areas, as well as those who have been concerned with a historical approach to Durkheim's work.

In the upsurge of interest in Durkheim, one should not forget that, perhaps following the initiative of Lukes, a centre in the

Maison des Sciences de l'Homme in Paris was created in 1975 for the study of Durkheim and his disciples under the leadership of Philippe Besnard. It produced a *Bulletin d'Informations, Etudes durkheimiennes* for about ten years. When this journal ceased *Etudes Durkheimiennes/Durkheim Studies* was then published in the United States under the editorship of R. A. Jones. In 1991 The British Centre for Durkheimian Studies was inaugurated and in 1994 it took over the journal edited by R. A. Jones and started publishing it annually under the name *Durkheimian Studies/Etudes Durkheimiennes* (see Preface).

Scholars around the world, especially in the United States, France, Germany and Britain, continue to write books and articles about Durkheim in increasing numbers, as is evident from the selection of items published in this Collection. One of the reasons for the revived interest in Durkheim is that since the collapse of the Eastern Bloc and the demise of Marxism, Durkheim with his democratic liberal humanism has become increasingly acceptable. This is particularly the case as no other overwhelmingly dominant approach to sociology has emerged in recent times.

From this very brief and broad view of Durkheim's professional career and his present place in the academic world, we turn to certain personal issues that surrounded his life.

Matters relating to Durkheim's personal life concern his Jewish origins, his attitude to family life and women, his political commitment, and his mental health.

Some students of Durkheim, especially certain Americans, such as Lehmann and Mestrovic, have tried to show recently that certain concepts he used, such as the sacred and solidarity, are in fact Jewish ideas. Indeed, to understand Durkheim it is best if one is well versed in Jewish thought, for such a knowledge helps to 'explain' his approach to sociology. There are obviously certain correlations but direct connections are difficult to prove as Pickering has pointed out [Pickering]. What has to be taken on board is that many Jewish concepts are to be found in Christianity, for Christianity emerged as a Jewish sect. Durkheim was as much steeped in Christianity as in Judaism.

In another direction one can point to the fact that Durkheim had a wish to remain a 'hidden', highly assimilated Jew [Pickering] (and see Pickering 1998). However, he became much more 'open' during the First World War, not least for his work with Russian Jewish refugees. His position towards Judaism remained ambivalent to his dying days. Emancipation, granted to the Jews after the French Revolution, frequently created dilemmas arising out of the wish for assimilation.

How did Durkheim behave towards his family and towards women? This issue has arisen mainly because of feminist studies which began after the 1970s. The charge is that Durkheim upheld the notion of male dominance.[1] From various sources, including his writings and letters recently published, the fact is undeniable that he was very much a patriarchal figure and a staunch supporter of monogamous marriage and family life built around it. The family was to be protected by a rigid moral code and he looked with alarm on the growing rates of divorce and illegitimacy. His was a puritanical disposition. He upheld a sexual morality which was very close to that of the Catholic and Protestant churches. The husband, for Durkheim, was indeed the head of the family. He was opposed to his daughter, Marie, receiving a university education. His wife, Louise, copied some of her husband's manuscripts and helped him in proof-reading, not least *L'Année sociologique*. There was a very clear division of labour between husband and wife. Durkheim worked extremely hard and seldom spoke, it is said, except at meals. Indeed, it would seem that the home had certain characteristics of a monastic house. But in general Durkheim's attitudes to home-life were very much in keeping with the majority of middle-class Frenchmen of his time. Those who would criticize certain aspects of Durkheim's personal and family life, often do so in the light of today's standards. They believe he should have exhibited standards of practice that are held to be desirable at the present time. Does one condemn the work of great scholars for their attitudes to family life or sexual morals? Durkheim clung to the axiom of the necessity of monogamous, life-long marriage for the maintenance of a stable society, certainly in the west. And today, he is not alone in that.

A question that remains a subject of debate is Durkheim's noncommitment to a political party. Above all a liberal and democrat, he always avoided openly supporting the socialist party and derided his nephew for being too involved in left-wing politics [Durkheim's *Lettres* and Pickering]. It is now generally agreed that in his struggle to establish sociology as a university discipline he wanted to avoid criticism of any political affiliation (see Chapter 6 here).

Finally, a question that is now coming out in the open relates to Durkheim's mental health. There was little information about it until recently. There are strong hints in the *Lettres à Marcel Mauss.* Certainly whatever psychological problems he might have had were never severe enough for him to stand down from work for any significant time, unlike the sociologist with whom he is so often compared, Max Weber. There is no reference anywhere that he was ever referred to a psychiatrist or sent to a mental hospital. We know he worked extremely hard, especially when he was at Bordeaux and during the First World War, and he usually did some work on holiday. He was very self-disciplined and often spoke about feeling very tired, and even what we might call depressed. He admitted he was a pessimist. It might be said he had some kind of neurasthenia but a lack of details about his personal life prevents further investigation. Laurent Mucchielli has referred to it as a '*névrose créatrice*' (1998).

The cause of Durkheim's death in 1917 remains a mystery, although some help comes from the *Lettres*. It was known already but now is even more apparent that the death of his beloved son André, in the Balkans, made a severe toll on his will to live. But we know, also, that he had some physical trouble, the nature of which awaits further research. He did not die a happy man.

Note

1. An item by M. Gane relating to Durkheim's attitude to women has not been included in this collection since it appeared in vol. 5 (1995, p. 201) of *Critical Assessments*. See Roth in Chapter 6.

References

Durkheim, E. (1998a) *Emile Durkheim. Lettres à Marcel Mauss*, Présentées par P. Bernard et M. Fournier, Paris: Presses Universitaires de France.
Lukes, S. (1973) *Emile Durkheim. His Life and Work: A Historical and Critical Study*, London: Allen Lane.
Mucchielli, L. (1998) 'Autour de la "révelation" d'Emile Durkheim', in J. Carroy and N. Richard, *La Découverte et ses récits en sciences humaines*, Paris: L'Harmattan.
Parsons, T. (1937) *The Structure of Social Action*, New York: McGraw-Hill.
Pickering, W. S. F. and Martins, H. (eds) (1994) *Debating Durkheim*, London: Routledge.
Pickering, W. S. F. (1998) 'Mauss's Jewish Background: a biographical essay', in W. James and N. J. Allen (eds), *Marcel Mauss: A Centenary Volume*, New York: Berghahn Books.

Selected Items

Durkheim, E. (1998) 'Emile Durkheim: lettres à Marcel Mauss', Présentées par P. Bernard et M. Fournier, Paris: Presses Universitaires de France, pp. 78–9, 107–9, 133–6, 161–3, 224–6, 414–5, 437–8, 498–9, 507–9.
Karady, V. (1983) *The Durkheimians in academe: a reconsideration*, in P. Besnard (ed.), *The Sociological Domain*, Cambridge: Cambridge University Press, pp. 71–89.
Pickering, W. S. F. (1994) 'The Enigma of Durkheim's Jewishness', in W. S. F. Pickering and H. Martins (eds), *Debating Durkheim*, London: Routledge, pp. 10–39.

Chapter 2

General sociology

Mike Gane

Durkheim tried to establish the field and method of sociology in a series of investigations from the mid-1880s till his death in 1917. It is clear that he sought to pull together diverse studies that were already in train into the new domain of social science, as well as to initiate new studies from a base in that domain. Both of these efforts involved the elaboration of a complex and viable project which would be sophisticated enough to establish an intellectual division of labour against the spontaneous drift of scholarship inspired by individual ambition alone. The objective would be to organize scholars into specialist sub-disciplines while maintaining a general perspective on their fields and methods of study.

Durkheim's concern with the organization of sociology itself developed within a comprehensive vision for the way the sciences as a whole might develop. In his view there was a danger on the one hand in over-specialization if it led to fragmentation and dispersion, and in vague generalized metaphysical philosophizing on the other. The most fruitful approach was one where development of method would go hand in hand with investigations guided by a general frame and strategy of research. But there was no single established genre for the consideration of 'general' issues in sociology as Durkheim's own reflections took time to find a settled form. At one time he became involved in a dispute with Gaston Richard about the nature and content of such a domain. He suggested this was where broad philosophical concerns continued to linger in various ways – inevitably perhaps – into the age of scientific sociology. Such lingering modes of reflection nonetheless would eventually be transformed and directed towards that area of abstract sociology which would consider general laws (Durkheim 1895a/1982:180–94).[1]

Reviews of the general character, scope, and orientation of the Durkheimian school and its notions of the unity of the social sciences were undertaken on a regular basis. One of the most central was that part of the book review section of *L'Année sociologique* which was specifically devoted to 'General Sociology'. This had subsections on general conceptions, social theories, social psychology, social conditions of knowledge, etc. Nandan has remarked that in no other section of the journal were 'the rubrics subjected to as many formal changes, even mutilation and alteration, as in the section on general sociology' (Nandan 1980:61).

Durkheim also considered this issue in 1909 in a discussion of 'Sociology and the Social Sciences' originally published in a collection of papers on method in different disciplines (in Traugott 1978:71–90). In this essay he provided the following schema for the divisions in sociology:

SOCIAL MORPHOLOGY
(Geographical base/population density, dispersion)

SOCIAL PHYSIOLOGY
(Religion, Morality, Law, Economics, etc.)

GENERAL SOCIOLOGY

Durkheim says of this latter category:

> As different as the various classes of social facts may be, they are, nonetheless, only species of the same genus, what characterises the social fact *in abstracto*, and whether there are very general laws of which the very diverse laws established by the special sciences are only particular forms. This is the object of general sociology, just as general biology has as its object to reveal the most general properties and laws of life.
>
> (In Traugott 1978:82)

His conception here is strategic, for he stresses that the value of knowledge of the general aspects of sociology depends on the quality of the 'analyses from which it results'.

This, however, is only one of many versions of the importance of the 'general' level of knowledge, for Durkheim is also capable of arguing that the detailed individual analyses themselves also need to be guided and organized by longer term strategic conceptions. The way that the problem is posed by Durkheim, with its insistence on both division of labour and on forms of co-ordination to prevent dispersion and fragmentation, owes much to Comte and the Comtean tradition [Schmaus]. The discussion of abnormal forms of the division of labour in Durkheim's *The Division of Labour in Society* very precisely traces the theme of these abnormal forms in intellectual and scientific fields from Comte's initial theory and baptizes them as anomic (Durkheim 1893b:291–309). Durkheim was careful to disassociate himself from any oversimplified Comteanism either in striving for methodological unification across the sciences, or in thinking that sociology has but one single problem (in Traugott 1978:82). Nevertheless, he did to some extent fall into the same difficulty as Comte in defining the problem in this way, that is to vacillate between an emphasis on detailed investigation as the basis of the development of scientific knowledge, and also to insist that science could never be reduced to the increasing accumulation of such empirical knowledge (Durkheim 1895a:150ff).

This lack of a single, clear and stable definition of what constitutes 'general' sociology and what its functions are, has continued in later reviews of the scope of sociology. These have been undertaken in many different forms. They not only include considerations of the definitions of concept and method of sociology itself and its theories and methods [Isambert, Schmaus, Gane 1994]. They include those attempts to define a twentieth-century general paradigm for sociology [Ritzer and Bell], as well as those efforts to unify apparently discrepant founding traditions [Boudon], and reflections on the status of 'classic' texts within the corpus of modern sociology and their changing significance [Jones]. But discussions of issues that have been seen to fall under the rubric of 'general' sociology can also be found in those reflections on method which have implications for research strategy [Gane 1988], in the sociological analysis of 'human nature' [Hawkins], on specific problems such as the Durkheimian orientation to treat social facts 'as things' [Stedman Jones], or to investigate the sophistication of a Durkheimian study of a particular social issue in a way that reveals the larger frame [Jones].

The history of sociology from its nominal inception with Comte in the 1820s and 1830s reveals a recurring pattern of advance and consolidation, and this very anthology of writings is witness to the most recent cycle of sociological thought which can be said to have opened in the 1960s. It is clear that one aspect of this late twentieth-century episode is its attention to the problems raised under the important rubric 'general sociology'. When sociology was established as a popular and widely taught subject in universities and schools a core corpus of significant writings was identified. This new corpus established at the end of the 1960s focused on Marx, Weber and Durkheim as the key founders of the discipline. Each of these writers was seen as providing essential dimensions to the modern discipline in a space defined as essentially contested. A number of issues arose in this context: the problem of the precise nature of the contribution of each of these sociologists, the relation between them, the genealogy of their problematics, the implication of their work for a conception of human nature, and so on. Giddens in 1987 considered again the specific contributions of Durkheim and Weber and again was concerned to stress that although these writers were committed to sociology:

> we have to acknowledge the depth of the differences between their respective legacies ... By adopting a framework of positive method, the social sciences (for Durkheim) could recapitulate a similar

order of established findings to those achieved within the natural sciences. Weber's scepticism of this view, and his distaste for too programmatic a methodological position, distanced him quite irrevocably from any such aspirations.

(Giddens 1987:188–9)

Raymond Boudon more recently, reflecting something of the decline of Marx's influence, has asked whether there was a common paradigm in the sociological orientations of Durkheim and Weber (Boudon).

Anthony Giddens can be seen to have played a major role in the first stage of this enterprise and his work is represented in his introduction to *Emile Durkheim: Selected Writings* published in 1972 [Giddens]. This collection followed on the heels of Giddens' major work *Capitalism and Modern Social Theory: An Analysis of the Writings of Marx, Durkheim and Max Weber* published in 1971. It is evident from Giddens's observations that he regarded these writings as an attempt to show that there had developed serious misconceptions about Durkheim's project:

I have sought to rescue Durkheim as an historical thinker . . . Durkheim was *not* primarily concerned with the 'problem of order', but with the problem of 'the *changing* nature of order' in the context of a definite conception of social development.

(Giddens 1971:ix)

Giddens has also said that a new beginning was required: 'The debate has been a sterile one and it is increasingly apparent that social theory must move in a new direction' (1972:48). His 'Introduction' [1972], included here, must be counted one of the clearest and most accurate brief overviews of Durkheim's sociology we have.

Another major work on Durkheim appeared at this time, Steven Lukes' *Emile Durkheim His Life and Work: A Historical and Critical Study* (1973), which has become the standard biography of Durkheim. But together in a surprising development, Giddens and Lukes were, in the next decade, when social science was to fall into public disfavour, to make a major, sustained, and completely misconceived, assault on Durkheim's methodology and sociology, particularly its general sociology. In his *New Rules of Sociological Method*, Giddens wrote that:

> many have ... relinquished the belief, for various reasons, that social science, in the near future, will be able to match the precision or the explanatory scope of even the less advanced natural sciences ... those who wait for a Newton are not only waiting for a train that won't arrive, they're in the wrong station altogether.
>
> (1976:13)

Lukes' own rejection of Durkheim's orientation was condensed into his 'Introduction' to Durkheim's *The Rules of Sociological Method* which had been re-translated in 1982 (1895a:1–27). In it he wrote that Durkheim's methodological essay was a 'clear statement of the aspiration towards a social science that is absolutely objective, specific (to social reality) and autonomous (of non-scientific influences), and a demonstration of why that aspiration was, and must remain, frustrated' (in Durkheim 1895a/t.1982:23). The discussion over the general programme of Durkheim had taken a very dramatic turn as Giddens and Lukes began to reject its fundamental theoretical ambitions.

In June 1981, the important American journal *Social Forces* devoted a special issue to Durkheimian sociology (vol. 59, no. 4). One of the contributions was a consideration of general sociology written by two leading American sociologists George Ritzer and Richard Bell. They asked, was Durkheim's programme an 'Exemplar for an Integrated Sociological Paradigm?' Their view was that Durkheim's work does not offer an adequate paradigm, and their argument was close to that developed by Giddens in his *New Rules*. They concluded that 'the thrust of his work leads to a passive image of the actor while an active actor is, in our view, an essential component of an integrated sociological paradigm' (Ritzer and Bell). In their conclusion they draw up a balance sheet. The positive aspects in Durkheim's theory were fivefold: its sense of multiple levels of social reality, sub-levels within them, insight into the interrelationships between them, analysis of the macro-subjective level, and a sense of the historical nature of the complex social whole. But there were seven negative elements in the theory: overemphasis of macro-subjective level, downgrading of other levels (micro-objective level unexplored), confusion of macro and micro levels with respect to the collective conscience, human nature left unexplored, narrow conception of method, 'too much attention on the macroscopic level and on reforms that needed to be made at that level', and a tendency to think in terms of one-way causation. Certainly it is not altogether clear whether the notion of an 'integrated sociological paradigm' is roughly equivalent to Durkheim's 'general sociology' for Durkheim thought more in terms of the latter in relation to the intellectual division of labour, rather than a formal set of abstract analytical categories (macro, micro, etc.) combined with philosophical concerns such as the conception of human nature.

There seemed to be two main sources of resistance to the increasingly hostile attitude to Durkheim which developed in the 1970s and early 1980s. One was the growth of serious interest in Durkheim's analysis of ritual, symbolic systems, the sociology of knowledge and the duality of human nature, which occupied Durkheim in *The Elementary Forms of the Religious Life* (1912a) in particular. This might be thought to have been of interest mainly to anthropologists, but this was not the case (one of the sociologists whose work is deeply indebted to this problematic was Erving Goffman). The other source was an increasing interest in the complexities of Durkheim's methodology, its sources in the French tradition, and its influence and effect on structuralism (anthropological, sociological and Marxist).

It is clear, then, that Durkheim did think about, reflect upon, and write about human nature and culture particularly in the later phase of his career. This was the topic examined in 1977 by Hawkins who argued that a close reading of Durkheim's work showed that his views changed fundamentally on these issues over time [Hawkins]. Durkheim did not have a crude set of fixed presuppositions about the individual, or about the nature of the social, external to and governing key orientations in his sociology. Rather, as his research developed so too did the sophistication of some of his more general ideas and orientations. In the 1980s there was also the beginning of reconsideration and defence of Durkheim's sociology at a much higher level of sophistication, a reaction to some of the gross oversimplifications of the attacks. In France, Isambert examined the subtleties of Durkheim's considerations of definitions, categories, and the distinction between common and scientific concepts [Isambert]. Another example was Warren Schmaus' significant discussion of Durkheim's sociological methodology as arising in debate with the Comtean tradition ([Schmaus], later developed in Schmaus 1994, especially chapter 5). And in 1988 two essays appeared independently on Durkheim's *Rules*, Berthelot's introduction to an annotated edition in France (see Durkheim 1895a, and Berthelot 1995), and Gane in Britain. Both essays sought to question the oversimplified and reductive readings of Durkheim's methodological ideas. One aspect of this new kind of discussion was to examine in a more balanced way what Durkheim meant by describing the development of the social sciences within the Enlightenment project as a 'complex transition' [Gane 1988]. The positive response to the attack by Giddens and Lukes on Durkheim's idea of the social fact has been to recover both its sophistication, effectiveness and its roots. This has been undertaken in diverse ways. The philosophical debt Durkheim owed to Renouvier when he coined the instruction that the social fact should be treated 'as a thing' is expounded by Stedman Jones [Stedman Jones].

Every so often sociologists reflect on the status of classic texts and attempt to explain their continuing attraction. In 1981 Buford Rhea collected together papers on *The Future of the*

Sociological Classics, which included Edward Tiryakian's essay 'Durkheim's *Elementary Forms* as "Revelation"1' (Rhea 1981:114–35), and in 1997 Charles Camic collected papers on *Reclaiming the Sociological Classics: The State of the Scholarship*, which included Robert Alun Jones' 'The Other Durkheim: History and Theory in the Treatment of Classical Sociological Thought' (Jones). It is interesting that both of these reflections on classical theory focus their attention on Durkheim's study *The Elementary Forms of the Religious Life* (1912a) and its meaning for Durkheim in the context of the Third Republic, and at the same time for sociologists today in a debate with Durkheim as our contemporary.

Jones argues that revisiting or working with classic sociological texts is not about, or should not be about, 'reclaiming' universal timeless arguments. In his analysis Durkheim's own practice was not to attempt to read classics in order to restate and then 'claim' their theoretical position or empirical findings. Durkheim's own readings and re-readings were often contradictory and incomplete, because they were positioned from within a set of changing problems in the present. Thus it is important to learn something about Durkheim's own practice, that 'timeless and universal truths often prove to be contingent and arbitrary, that the forms of intellectual life are infinitely various, that history itself is deeply ironic and therefore occasionally quite humbling' [Jones].

It is in the light of these comments that it would be possible to make a reconsideration of Durkheim's idea of a 'general sociology' today. Its scope would probably be somewhat wider than the conception Durkheim presented in his discussion of 1909, i.e. that it would be the synthesis of empirical studies in order to generate general laws. It would not follow the Comtean model of the specification of sociological method as one aspect of the positive methods of the sciences in general. It seems clear from the items selected for this section that the word 'general' would include aspects of philosophy, method, and history of sociology. It also includes all those moments where sociologists ask questions about what they have done, where they have come from and where they are going.

Note

1. In references relating to Durkheim, the first number is the dating-enumeration of the work according to Lukes 1973. Where a page number follows after a / , the number refers to the corresponding page number in the translation stated in the details of the entry under Durkheim's dating-enumeration in the references below. (See Referencing.)

References

Berthelot, J.-M. (1995) *1895 Durkheim: L'Avenement de la Sociologie Scientifique*, Toulouse: Presses Universitaires du Mirail.

Durkheim, E. (1893b) *De la Division du travail social*, Paris: Alcan.

— (t.1984) by W. D. Halls, *The Division of Labour in Society*, London: Macmillan.

— (1895a) *Les Règles de la méthode sociologique*, Paris: Alcan.

— (1988) Repr. with an Introduction by J.-M. Berthelot, Paris: Flammarion.

— (t.1982) by W. D. Halls, with Introduction by S. Lukes, *The Rules of Sociological Method*, London: Macmillan.

— (1912a) *Les Formes élémentaires de la vie religieuse*, Paris: Alcan.

— (t.1995) by K. Fields, *The Elementary Forms of Religious Life*, New York: The Free Press.

Gane, M. (1988) *On Durkheim's Rules of Sociological Method*, London: Routledge.

Giddens, A. (1971) *Capitalism and Modern Social Theory. An Analysis of the Writings of Marx, Durkheim and Weber*, Cambridge: Cambridge University Press.

Giddens, A. (1972) *Emile Durkheim: Selected Writings*, Cambridge: Cambridge University Press.

Giddens, A. (1976) *New Rules of Sociological Method*, London: Hutchinson.

Giddens, A. (1987) 'Weber and Durkheim: Coincidence and Divergence', in W. Mommsen and J. Osterhammel (eds), *Max Weber and his Contemporaries*, London: Allen & Unwin.

Nandan, Y. (ed.) (1980) *Emile Durkheim: Contributions to L'Année sociologique*, London: Collier-Macmillan.

Rhea, B. (ed.) (1981) *The Future of the Sociological Classics*, London: Allen & Unwin.

Schmaus, W. (1985) 'Hypotheses and Historical Analysis in Durkheim's Sociological Methodology: A Comtean Tradition', *Studies in History and Philosophy of Science* 16:1–30.

Schmaus, W. (1994) *Durkheim's Philosophy of Science and the Sociology of Knowledge*, Chicago: University of Chicago Press.

Traugott, M. (ed.) (1978) *Emile Durkheim on Institutional Analysis*, Chicago: University of Chicago Press.

Selected Items

Boudon, R. (1995) 'Weber and Durkheim: beyond the differences: a common important paradigm?', *Revue International de Philosophie* 192:221–39.

Gane, M. (1994) 'A fresh look at Durkheim's sociological method', in W. S. F. Pickering and H. Martins (eds), *Debating Durkheim*, London: Routledge.

Gane, M. (1988) 'Complex transitions', in Mike Gane, *On Durkheim's Rules of Sociological Method*, London: Routledge.

Giddens, A. (1972) 'Introduction: Durkheim's writings in sociology and social philosophy', in A. Giddens, *Emile Durkheim: Selected Writings*, Cambridge: Cambridge University Press.

Hawkins, M. J. (1977) 'A re-examination of Durkheim's theory of human nature', *Sociological Review* 25:29–52.

Isambert, F.-A. (1982) 'De la Définition: réflexions sur la stratégie durkheimienne de détermination de l'objet', *L'Année sociologique* 32:163–92.

Jones, R. A. (1997) 'The other Durkheim: history and theory in the treatment of classical sociological thought', in C. Camic (ed.), *Reclaiming the Sociological Classics: the state of scholarship*, Oxford: Blackwell.

Ritzer, G. and Bell, R. (1981) 'Emile Durkheim: exemplar for an integrated sociological paradigm?', *Social Forces* 59(4):966–95.

Schmaus, W. (1985) 'Hypotheses and historical analysis in Durkheim's sociological methodology: a Comtean tradition', *Studies in the History and Philosophy of Science* 16(1):1–30.

Stedman Jones, S. (1996) 'What does Durkheim mean by "thing"?', *Durkheimian Studies/Etudes Durkheimiennes* 2:43–59.

Chapter 3

Religion

W. S. F. Pickering

Today, when traditional religion and indeed religious life in general finds only a limited place in western society and in other societies influenced by it, it seems strange to find that the section here on religion has such a prominent position. And all the more so since the author in question was of Jewish background, the son of a rabbi and who abandoned all religious belief at the age of late adolescence. He became a thoroughly convinced rationalist-humanist, almost an atheist (see Pickering 1984:5–13). Yet the fact remains that Durkheim gave religion a prominent place in his attempt to offer a scientific explanantion of social phenomena.

However, it was not just a matter of saying that religion was important in social life in what one might crudely call quantitative terms, but that religion in itself was the key to the scientific understanding of society. It was, as he said, the *clef de voûte* of social life. Hence, in approaching any society the focal point of study should be its religion. Through representations (beliefs and ideals) and actions (rituals), other institutions such as the family, morals, etc. can be understood. Durkheim went as far as to say that in the beginning 'all was religious'.

The fervour with which Durkheim pursued his professional task and the remarkable place he accorded religion in his system of thought has made one commentator at least see his life and work as something akin to a religious quest (see Pickering 1984).

How did this all come about? In 1895 Durkheim, on his own confession, experienced something of an academic revelation: one might say a conversion. He had always been convinced that religion had an important place in society but as a result of reading the work of William Robertson Smith, the Presbyterian, Old Testament scholar with an interest in anthropology, he became certain that religion was the key to understanding society sociologically (Pickering 1984:60–70). What exactly caused the change, be it the notion of the sacred, the importance of ritual, or even totemism, remains a matter of speculation among scholars. It took Durkheim just under twenty years to produce a book on religion which was to crown his academic achievements, *Les Formes élémentaires* (1912a; see Allen *et al.* 1998).

His conviction over the centrality of religion in any objective understanding of society, meant that when he created the *Année sociologique*, the first volume of which appeared in 1898, the subject of religion constituted the second section, having been preceded by that of general sociology. From then until the last issue in 1913, the twelfth volume, 'religion' remained the largest and most important of all the sections. Part of a letter to Mauss firmly underlines this:

> *L'Année sociologique* doit marquer une orientation. Au fond cette importance sociologique du phénomène religieux est l'aboutissement de tout ce que j'ai fait; et cela a l'avantage de résumer toute notre orientation d'une manière concrète, plus concrète que les formules que j'ai employées jusqu'à présent.
>
> (Durkheim 1998a:91).

To many academics of his day, Durkheim's position seemed, if not outrageous then very questionable. Not surprisingly, he was attacked by two diametrically opposed groups. Those, who were 'believers', whether Catholic or Protestant, denounced Durkheim for reducing religion to its social component and denying the existence of a god or God. In emphasizing the social, the most important element was seen by them to be omitted, namely the individual or spiritual components. Amongst such critics one may point to the attack by Durkheim's former colleague, Gaston Richard, whose criticisms are many and wide-ranging [Richard].[1] It was over the question of religion that Richard left the Année Sociologique group of which he was a senior member. Criticisms of reductionism, in making religion a human activity as well as a social phenomenon, have also recently been made by Hamnett [Hamnett].

At the opposite end of the spectrum were thorough-going rationalists who held that either religion was an illusion, an ideology in the Marxist sense, or those who, on strictly scientific grounds, were convinced of the secondary role of religion in society. Amongst the latter, one might refer to Gustave Belot who held that religion was derived from ethics, whereas Durkheim held that the opposite was the case (Belot 1907; 1913).

Durkheim's *via media* position is abundently clear in his assertion that religion was a reality or real force – a force because it exerted an influence over people. This is nowhere more evident than in the extemporaneous talk he gave in 1913 at a conference of *Libres Penseurs et Libres Croyants* (Durkheim 1919b). The believers and non-believers could both come together in seeing the social reality of religion.

It should be noted that not all Durkheim's disciples followed him in his stand over religion. Marcel Mauss who wrote more extensively on the subject than any other follower was not as convinced as Durkheim that religion should be given a prime place above all other social institutions. His approach was less essentialist in the matter of the use of the sacred than that of Durkheim (Martelli 1993:378–9) and his interest in religion appeared to wane after Durkheim died, to judge at least by the number of his publications on the subject (see Pickering 1998).

After Durkheim's death in 1917 studies in religion in France that attempted to extend and refine his ideas, developed hardly at all. It would seem that such followers as Durkheim had in this period wished to forget his contributions to the study of religion. The one exception was the Collège de Sociologie associated with the names of Bataille and Callois but its influence was very limited. Books by Durkheim other than *The Elementary Forms of the Religious Life* were of greater concern. This trend continued in the years that followed World War II, save for the important work of Claude Lévi-Strauss in developing theories of myth based on structuralism [Hamnett]. In this he acknowledged the thinking of Durkheim and Mauss. Anthropologists in France and elsewhere have on the whole found the ideas of Mauss more helpful in their work than the wider, more generalizing theories of Durkheim (Martelli 1993).

Durkheim stamped his thought on the sociological study of religion by insisting that the sacred is central to religion – sacred beliefs and sacred actions involving people in a social group (see Isambert 1982:213–99). He defined the sacred as that which is inviolable – that which is impossible to go beyond, for it relates to the ultimate – the ultimate as determined by a society. Today there are many scholars who continue to find the concept helpful in analysing both religion and society. And it can be applied, for example, to new religions or religious movements in which the sacred continues to have a place. One example given here relates to the emergence of new religions at the time of the French Revolution [Hunt]. Again, it appears in the notion of social memory which creates new national holidays. In recent times in Germany problems have arisen in connection with such festivities [Gephart].

On the other hand, there have been critics of the concept of the sacred from Durkheim's time to the present. These have questioned its value, especially as it is linked in Durkheim's thought with the concept of the profane, which is a much more difficult concept to handle, since it stands near to but is not identical with the secular or the 'ordinary'. Another problem turns on whether what is sacred is religious and whether the religious can be equated with what is sacred. According to Durkheim the notion of the sacred, but not the particular contents of the sacred, is universal and he goes further and holds that the sacred is necessary for a society to exist. Is it religion in the traditional sense or the sacred which is a prerequisite for a society? Clearly it is the sacred since every religion is based on it. What if the sacred in a society is difficult or impossible to locate empirically, for instance in a thoroughly secular society? Further, can a 'secular' sacred perform the same functions as a religion as generally conceived? These issues are raised by Pickering where the eternality of the sacred is questioned on empirical grounds in certain modern western societies [Pickering] (see also Martelli 1993:376–9). The sacred is not sacred universally.

One great contribution that Durkheim made to the study of religion was to emphasize the importance of ritual as being complementary to belief – each undergirded or reinforced the other. Which was prior logically or historically remains a matter for debate: perhaps it is an impossible question to answer (see Pickering 1984:ch.20). Certain anthropologists, especially in Britain, have seized on ritual or religious action as being the most significant element in religion. One reason at least for holding to such a position is that, compared with beliefs, ritual is easy to locate emprirically. But there has been a tendency to extend the analysis by asserting that ritual is the main cohesive force at work in preliterate societies. In fact, in their hands ritual becomes equivalent to religion. Malcolm Ruel would challenge this position and assert that in Durkheim beliefs – religious representations – are just as important in Durkheim's analysis as is ritual [Ruel]. The question of priority is again not solved. And the fundamental question remains – if it can be said that a society is integrated or creates its own social order, what is the instrument of achievement? Ritual, belief, or something else, perhaps a combination of factors?

Raymond Boudon in a recent article on *Les Formes élémentaires* fails to consider ritual or its relation to religious beliefs but he shows the importance of Durkheim's theory of such beliefs as part of beliefs in general (collective representations) (Boudon 1999:171–79). He is not alone in drawing attention to the value of Durkheim's concept of the soul as a symbolic response to the reality of the dualism of the individual and the social within the person and their relation to society (ibid.:179–85).

To a thinker such as Durkheim, who denied the truth-value of any religion, the virtue of religion is its symbolic system. Symbolism is central to a society and it is the symbols of the religion which really do 'the work'. Arguing from totemic beliefs and practices, the most significant contribution Durkheim made in his classic *Les Formes élémentaires*, was what he said about symbolism. The relevant chapter in the centre of the book is carefully expounded here by Paoletti, who raises amongst other issues the nature of symbolism itself [Paoletti]. According to Durkheim the objects, such as plants and animals, are less important than their symbols, which become the focus of worship and religious action. In order to study religion one needs to penetrate the reality represented by the symbol. As for society, so for religion: it is a system of symbols. But here again stands the danger of confusing, ontologically, religion with society (see Pickering 1984:ch.14). Ôno holds that society in Durkheim's eyes is essentially a religious phenomenon [Ôno]. Society is supported by a supra-individual, non-rational, non-cognitive factor, religion itself, expressed in terms of the sacred.

But how do symbols, basic ideas and ideals change? For change they do. Durkheim, concerned with this problem as much as that of the stability of a society, deduced from his study of Australian aboriginals that change could occur through effervescent assemblies (see Pickering 1984:chs 21 and 22). In such gatherings, when many social controls are lifted, unexpected outcomes emerge, such as new concepts, values, and beliefs. In recent times, largely forgotten though it has been in the past, the concept has turned out to be profitable. The precise techniques of the process, however, remain hidden (see the reference to Tiryakian in Chapter 6). Further, occasions of effervescent excitement are re-enacted ritually to reinforce the new representations created on the first occasion. Ever since Durkheim first developed the idea, it has been attacked on account of its psychological mechanisms. Pickering has tried to show that these early attacks were not justified and that Durkheim was able to keep the concept within sociological bounds. However, one scholar has recently challenged this in pointing to the emotional component of the process [Mellor]. The anthropologist, N. Allen, has found that effervescent gatherings through their creative function could have been instrumental in bringing about social life [Allen]. He notes that something akin to social effervescence is found amongst apes and, with them as with humans, it may be accompanied by active sexual behaviour.

It was not Durkheim's intention in writing *Les Formes élémentaires* to deal with contemporary religion in the western world. Such, however, was his deep interest in religion that he could not avoid extrapolating the contemporary state of religion from his consideration of preliterate religion. In his eyes traditional religions in the west were effete. In their place a new religion was emerging without a personal deity in which man became the cult of man. For Durkheim this solved the problem of the eternality of religion as a necessary component of all social life. At the centre of this new and destined-to-become universal religion were beliefs in the rights of man [Filloux]. The cult of the individual lacks meaningful rituals and symbols and in the end, it can be argued, becomes a system of ethics without a transcendental base. Nevertheless, many scholars today see it as the religion of contemporary western society.

By developing *sociologie religieuse*, as Durkheim called it, he deserves the title of co-founder of the sociology of religion, along with Max Weber. Today the sociology of religion at the level of general theory has not greatly advanced in any agreed manner (Martelli 1993:375). Sociology of religion is, however, finding Durkheim's concepts valuable in examining new religious trends in society such as secular religions, so-called fundamentalism, New Age movements, syncretism, religio-national movements, contemporary symbolism and so on (see especially the work of Ken Thompson in Thompson 1993; 1998).

No student today can avoid coming to terms with the contributions Durkheim made in the realm of religion, where he did not distinguish sociology from anthropology [Hamnett].

Note

1. Although this is a relatively old publication in terms of these volumes, it has long been neglected. For further information about Richard, see Pickering 1975:343–59.

References

Allen, N. J., Pickering, W. S. F. and Watts Miller, W. (eds) (1998) *On Durkheim's Elementary Forms of Religious Life*, London: Routledge.

Belot, G. (1907) *Etudes de morale positive*, Paris: Alcan.

Belot, G. (1913) 'Une théorie nouvelle de la religion', *Revue philosophique* 75:329–79.

Boudon, R. (1999) '*Les Formes élémentaires de la vie religieuse*: une théorie toujours vivante', *L'Année sociologique* 49(1):149–98.

Durkheim, E. (1912a) *Les Formes élémentaires de la vie religieuse. Le système totémique en Australie*, Paris: Alcan.

Durkheim, E. (1919b) Contribution to discussion in F. Abouzit *et al.*, *Le Sentiment religieux à l'heure actuelle*, Paris: Vrin.

Durkheim, E. (1998a) Emile Durkheim. *Lettres à Marcel Mauss*, Paris: Presses Universitaires de France.

Isambert, F.-A. (1982) *Le Sens du sacré*, Paris: Les Editions du Minuit

Martelli, S. (1993) 'Mauss et Durkheim: un désaccord sur la question du sacré et une perspective relationnelle sur Simmel et la société post-moderne', *Social Compass* 40(3):175–87.

Pickering, W. S. F. (1975) *Durkheim on Religion*, London: Routledge and Kegan Paul.

Pickering, W. S. F. (1984) *Durkheim's Sociology of Religion. Themes and Theories*, London: Routledge and Kegan Paul.

Pickering, W. S. F. (1998) 'Mauss's Jewish Background: A Biographical Essay', in W. James and N. J. Allen (eds), *Marcel Mauss: A Centenary Volume*, New York: Berghahn.

Thompson, K. (1993) 'Durkheim, Ideology and the Sacred', *Social Compass* 40(3):451–61.

Thompson, K. (1998) 'Durkheim and Sacred Identity', in N. J. Allen, W. S. F. Pickering and W. Watts Miller (eds) (1998) *On Durkheim's Elementary Forms of Religious Life*, London: Routledge.

Selected Items

Allen, N. J. (1998) 'Effervescence and the origins of human society', in N. J. Allen, W. S. F. Pickering and W. Watts Miller (eds), *On Durkheim's Elementary Forms of Religious Life*, London: Routledge.

Filloux, J.-C. (1990) 'Personne et sacré chez Durkheim', *Archives de sciences sociales des religions* 69:41–53.

Gephart, W. (1998) 'Memory and the sacred: the cult of anniversaries and commemorative rituals in the light of *The Elementary Forms*', in N. J. Allen, W. S. F. Pickering and W. Watts Miller (eds), *On Durkheim's Elementary Forms of Religious Life*, London: Routledge.

Hamnett, I. (1984) 'Durkheim and the study of religion', in S. Fenton (ed.), *Durkheim and Modern Sociology*, Cambridge: Cambridge University Press.

Hunt, L. (1988) 'The sacred and the French Revolution', in J. C. Alexander (ed.), *Durkheimian Sociology: Cultural Studies*, Cambridge: Cambridge University Press.

Mellor, P. A. (1998) 'Sacred contagion and social vitality: collective effervescence in *Les Formes élémentaires de la vie religieuse*', *Durkheimian Studies/Etudes Durkheimiennes* 4:87–114.

Ôno, M. (1996) 'Collective effervescence and symbolism', *Durkheimian Studies/Etudes Durkheimiennes*, n.s., 2:79–98.

Paoletti, G. (1998) 'The cult of images: reading Chapter VII, Book II, of *The Elementary Forms*', in N. J. Allen, W. S. F. Pickering and W. Watts Miller (eds), *On Durkheim's Elementary Forms of Religious Life*, London: Routledge.

Pickering, W. S. F. (1990) 'The Eternality of the sacred: Durkheim's error?', *Archives de sciences sociales des religions* 69:91–108.

Richard, G. (1975) 'Dogmatic atheism in the sociology of religion', in W. S. F. Pickering, (ed.) *Durkheim on Religion*, London: Routledge & Kegan Paul.

Ruel, M. (1998) 'Rescuing Durkheim's "rites" from the symbolizing anthropologists', in N. J. Allen, W. S. F. Pickering and W. Watts Miller (eds), *On Durkheim's Elementary Forms of Religious Life*, London: Routledge.

Chapter 4

Epistemology and philosophy of science

Warren Schmaus

The relation between epistemology and philosophy of science

Today, philosophers look upon epistemology and the philosophy of science as closely related disciplines that are both concerned with questions about the justification of knowledge claims. Durkheim, however, appears to have regarded them as distinct. In his lectures on philosophy given towards the beginning of his career at the Lycée de Sens (1996a), he treated philosophy of science, or 'methodology' as he called it, as a part of applied logic. Epistemology or theory of knowledge, on the other hand, was considered under the rubric of 'psychology'. French academic philosophy at that time followed the Cartesian tradition of beginning with an introspective inquiry into the human mind. This philosophical psychology was supposed to provide the foundation for all of philosophy, including metaphysics, morals, and even logic. In fact, following his fellowship year in Germany, Durkheim reported that he was 'astonished' to learn that the Germans had an entirely different conception of philosophy (1887a:324). German students of philosophy began their studies with logic, which for them included epistemology. Psychology was regarded as a closely related but distinct discipline.

A central issue in French epistemology in Durkheim's day was that of the origin of our most fundamental categories of thought, including space, time, causality, and substance.

Although these bore some resemblance to the Kantian categories, the French tended to treat them as akin to the abstract general ideas of pre-critical philosophy. They sought the origins of these concepts in experience, thinking that this constituted a 'scientific' approach to philosophy. Durkheim's later sociology of knowledge, represented by *The Elementary Forms of Religious Life* (1912a) and 'Primitive Classification' (1903a(i)), was very much a part of a movement in France that was attempting to 'naturalize' a theory of the categories, that is, to treat it according to the empirical methods of the natural sciences. He differed from his philosophical contemporaries largely in proposing social in place of psychological causes and origins for the categories.

Durkheim's writings in the philosophy of science, such as *The Rules of Sociological Method* (1895a), at first appear to be unrelated to his epistemology. The normative content of his rules of method derives from his conception of the aims of inquiry, not from his theory of the categories. However, just to the extent he was attempting to naturalize epistemology, his philosophy of science becomes relevant to his epistemology. That is, if we are to interpret his epistemology as a scientific theory, it makes sense to do so in the light of his conception of science.

Whether a naturalized epistemology such as Durkheim's carries any normative implications for what should count as knowledge remains an open question for us today. It is analogous to the problem Durkheim faced in his project of establishing ethics on a sociological basis. Around the turn of the century, the philosopher G. E. Moore dismissed such projects for committing what he called the 'naturalistic fallacy', that is, the fallacy of attempting to derive a normative 'ought' statement from a descriptive 'is' statement. However, it is not entirely clear that the naturalistic fallacy really is a fallacy. As one contemporary naturalist, Larry Laudan (1990), has argued, although all general inferences from experience may be deductive fallacies, there is no reason to think that good reasoning is exhausted by deduction.

The reception of Durkheim's philosophical views

The way in which one interprets Durkheim's methodology and epistemology has implications for the way in which one understands his sociology (see Chapter 10). For this reason, readings of his philosophical views have been highly contentious. Social scientists have tended either to enlist Durkheim in support of their agenda or to castigate him as a paragon of wrong-headed 'positivism'. Notoriously, Parsons (1937) and more recently Alexander (1982) regard Durkheim as having undergone a shift from his early 'positivist' concern with causes in the material world to a more mentalistic concern with norms and values in his later sociology (see Chapter 10). Other theorists, such as J. Douglas (1967), Hirst (1975), Taylor (1982), Johnson *et al.* (1984), Gane (1988), and Boudon (1995) read *The Rules* as endorsing a naive empiricism that they find to be at variance with Durkheim's more rationalist procedures in his substantive works such as *Suicide* (1897a).

What many interpreters of Durkheim's philosophy of science overlook is that *The Rules* only appears to be empiricist because it is an eclectic work [Brooks] (1998). Insofar as it is eclectic, it is just as rationalist as empiricist. The very title of the book alludes to Descartes's *Rules for the Direction of the Mind* (1628). Durkheim's eclecticism makes it possible for others, such as Alpert (1961), Wallwork (1972), Lukes (1973, 1982), Watts Miller (1993) [1996], Jones [1994] (1996), and Schmaus (1994; 1995) to interpret him as a rationalist, a realist, and even an essentialist.

In my book of 1994, I show that Durkheim endorsed a method that is the very antithesis of positivism. He sought causal explanations, which have been opposed by positivists since Auguste Comte. In a manner that is inconsistent with the positive philosophy, he posited that there are real kinds of social phenomena and sought explanations of these phenomena in terms of their underlying real essences. For Durkheim, social phenomena are to be explained ultimately in terms of such unobservable entities as collective representations and social forces, which positivism would rule out. As he explained in the preface to the second edition to *The Rules* (1901c), social constraint is to be explained in terms of the coercive power that certain representations have over us.

Lukes however tends to regard the concept of collective representations as belonging to a later development in Durkheim's thought (1973; 1982). To be sure, although Durkheim used the term in his earliest publications from the 1880s, he did not appeal to it there as often as he did in his later works beginning in 1898. Nevertheless, the discovery of Durkheim's 1884 Sens lectures by Neil Gross in 1995 reveal that Durkheim was concerned from the very outset of his career with representations (Durkheim 1996a). Most tellingly, Durkheim specifically addressed in these lectures the issue of the relationship between representations and the categories (Schmaus 2000).

Gieryn (1982) and Jones [1994] suggest that the sociology of knowledge of Durkheim's later works (viz., 1903a(i) and 1912a) has conceptual relativist implications that undermine his philosophy of science, in particular his realism about kinds. That is, if the categories that shape experience are cultural constructions, then how can we say that the kinds of things into which we sort the objects of experience are real? Indeed, beginning with Mauss, there has been an ethnological tradition of giving a relativist reading to Durkheim's theory of the social causes of the categories. Some of Durkheim's earliest critics, such as Gehlke (1915), Goldenweiser (1915), Schaub (1920), and Dennes (1924), have seen the whole enterprise of providing social causes for the categories as either question-begging or as confusing categories with mental contents. Curiously, both relativists (Bloor 1982) and anti-relativists (Rawls 1997) have recently tried to defend Durkheim against these early critics. Others, however, including Lukes (1973) and Godlove (1986; 1989), have criticized Durkheim's theory of the categories for attempting to provide an empirical answer to a philosophical question, that is, for mixing factual issues of causes and origins with normative questions about justification. They also find Durkheim's arguments incoherent, insofar as he said that the categories are culturally variable and yet universal and necessary.

On the other hand, I have tried to find some consistency in Durkheim's thought. In my book, I argue that Durkheim's sociology of knowledge does not have the relativist implications that have been attributed to it and is thus consistent with his philosophy of science (Schmaus 1994). When interpreting his theory of the categories, one must be careful to recognize that, for Durkheim, there can be more than one collective representation of the same category and that it is these collective representations, not the categories, that are culturally variable. In some of my papers, I follow up this line of interpretation by arguing that what Durkheim in fact provides is a theory of the social functions of the categories and a theory of the social causes of their representations [Schmaus 1998; 2000b]. The categories take their meanings from the social functions they serve, which are necessary for social life and thus universally found in all societies. Yet the precise way in which these socially important concepts are represented may vary with local conditions.

Durkheim's philosophy of science

Several recent papers on Durkheim's philosophy of science, which I discuss below, go beyond a mere analysis of *The Rules* taken by itself and interpret his methodology in the context of his other writings and the philosophical tradition from which he emerged. This contextual reading sheds light on his philosophy of science in a way that helps us to clarify some of his arguments in his sociology of knowledge.

Brooks provides an interpretation of the *Rules* as an expression of the philosophy of science taught by the eclectic spiritualists (1996). He shows how *The Rules* follows the eclectics' standard textbook procedure of initiating a work of science with a provisional definition of its domain of facts expressed in terms of their external or observable characteristics. Watts Miller also recognizes that when Durkheim argued that social facts are things because they resist willed effort, he was writing for an audience of eclectic spiritualist philosophers [Watts Miller]. Cousin, the founder of this movement, promoted the philosophy of Maine de Biran, who had argued that our introspective experience of willed effort made possible our self-knowledge and our knowledge of the external world. Maine de Biran in turn drew this argument from a French philosophical tradition that began with Condillac and continued through the *idéologues* Cabanis and Destutt de Tracy.

Jones [1994] and Watts Miller [1996], like Schmaus [1994], turn to Durkheim's Latin dissertation on Montesquieu to support an essentialist reading of Durkheim. Jones also interprets Durkheim's dissertation as an attempt to come to terms with the Cartesian rationalist tradition that he shared with Montesquieu. He explains how Durkheim developed his concepts of social types and social volume through a critique of Montesquieu's similar concepts. Watts Miller shows that once we understand that Durkheim held an essentialist model of causation, in which causes are linked not just chronologically but logically to their effects, we can make better sense of his argument in *The Rules* against Mill on the plurality of causes. As Brooks has shown elsewhere, this argument, too, is hardly unique to Durkheim and can be found in eclectic spiritualist philosophy textbooks (1998:216; 295n.117).

An appreciation of Durkheim's essentialism is important for interpreting his sociological works. To provide an essentialist explanation of a fact is to show how it strives to express its nature and fulfill its function. For an essentialist like Durkheim, as Watts Miller explains, a functional explanation seems to be a type of causal explanation. Although Durkheim may have distinguished causal from functional explanation in *The Rules*, the more important distinction for him was that between causal explanations and intentional explanations, which appeal to agents' reasons. Hence, in his sociological works, Durkheim did not always carefully maintain the distinction between functional and causal explanations. This lack of a clear separation between these two kinds of explanation has led to an ambiguity in his account of the division of labor. Many have read him as having said that it is caused by factors in the physical environment. However, he can just as easily be read as having said that it is an functional adaptation to such factors (Schmaus 1994, 1995). A similar ambiguity can be found in his sociological theory of the categories in *The Elementary Forms of Religious Life* (1912a), in which the claim that they depend on social causes has been combined with the argument that they evolved to make social life possible.

Durkheim's sociology of knowledge

The presence of controversy can both mask and reveal the existence of a considerable agreement. It is precisely when the disputants agree on so much that they argue so vehemently over that about which they disagree. This is surely the case with the controversy between Rawls [1996; 1998] and me [Schmaus 1998] over the interpretation of Durkheim's theory of the categories. We agree that Durkheim was no relativist and that his goals were as much philosophical as sociological. We also agree that his theory of the categories is contained not just in the introduction and conclusion to *The Elementary Forms* and that his account of the concepts of causality, force, and power in the middle of the book is fundamental to the whole theory. We disagree, however, over whether Durkheim's attempt to justify the categories is a causal or a functional account and whether a causal account can succeed as a normative epistemology. Rawls shares Durkheim's assumption that epistemology is concerned with the origins of the contents of the human mind. She holds that for Durkheim, not only was the category of causality derived from the experience of social forces, but that this origin somehow validated the concept. I, on the other hand, hold that the very idea that we can experience forces, as opposed to their effects, is idiosyncratic to the eclectic spiritualists, with their fixation on willed effort. Also, I claim that questions about origins have more to do with semantics or the meanings of our concepts than with the validation of knowledge in the first place.

Rawls seems to think that when I use the term 'semantics', I am referring only to a twentieth century invention that begins and ends with something like Quine's notion that the meaning of a concept is given by its network of relationships with other concepts. This reading disregards not only the more recent turn to causal theories in semantics, but also the fact that the semantic turn in philosophy goes back at least to Hobbes and characterizes much of British empiricism. Hume, for instance, in the *Enquiry Concerning Human Understanding*, proposed that when we suspect that a philosophical term is being used 'without any meaning' we should investigate its origins (1966: 22). Then, in the fourth section, he makes the *epistemological* point that – contra Rawls – general causal claims *cannot* be inferred from experience. This leads him in the seventh section to an investigation of what can then be the source and hence the *meaning* of the concept of causation.

Rawls also does not appreciate my reasons for thinking that an appeal to the social causes of the categories does not necessarily explain their necessity and universality and hence cannot defeat a relativist interpretation of Durkheim. She thinks that when I argue that such an account leaves the categories merely contingent, that I am objecting to the *social* aspect of social causes. On the contrary, it is the *causal*-aspect of social causes that troubles me. Unless these causes are themselves necessary, that which depends on them must be contingent. However, if social causes vary with local circumstances, they are not necessary but contingent causes. Durkheim explained the universality and necessity of the categories by appealing to their necessary social *functions*, not their contingent social causes. Rawls herself, towards the end of her second paper, gives a functional account of the categories when she says that groups that do not form these concepts do not become societies. She also misreads me when she says that I favor an 'a priori' account of the categories: a functional account is just as much a naturalized account as is a causal account of the categories.

In her interpretation of Durkheim's theory of the categories, Rawls assumes a univocal concept of causality, one that combines force, power, and necessary connection, and seeks a common origin for all these ideas. Durkheim, however, broke with a philosophical tradition that goes back at least to Hume by introducing a distinction between the idea of necessary connection and the idea of force or power and assigning separate origins to each idea. He traced the origin of our idea of power or force to our experience of social forces, in opposition to the animist theory of the origin of religion, which, like the eclectic spiritualist philosophy, traced it to our introspective experience of the activity of the will. He traced the origin of the idea of necessary connection, on the other hand, to the obligation of members of society to participate in its religious rites. In order for indigenous Australians to participate in certain totemic rites, he argued, they must believe that there is a necessary connection between their participation and the flourishing of the totemic species. As the idea of a necessary connection is presupposed by the very idea of obligation, it thus has the important social function of making moral rules possible [Schmaus]. However, only the idea of necessary connection and not the idea of force or power is presupposed by the idea of moral obligation and thus has this social function.

Of course, the mere functional necessity of a category such as causality by itself carries no normative weight. The justification of the categories would also require some argument to the effect that maintaining human society is a moral good. I believe that this is an argument that Durkheim was prepared to make. However, Durkheim's social functional account of the necessity and universality of the categories should not be confused with a pragmatic justification of them. Indeed, he vehemently defended a representational or correspondence notion of truth against the pragmatist theory of William James. Whereas for James, our ideas are true because they work, for Durkheim, they work because they are true. Gross argues that Durkheim associated James's pragmatism with Bergsonian spiritualism and Catholic modernism insofar as all these trends denied any intrinsic value to thought [Gross]. Durkheim felt that his own studies of religion had demonstrated that human beings have purely intellectual needs and thus that pragmatism and these allied philosophies were empirically false.

As I have indicated above, Durkheim held that there could be more than one collective representation of the same category. To say this much, however, is to raise the question as to what it is that could make several representations all instances of the same category. I would argue that what they have in common or what gives them their meaning is their social function. However, the structures of these representations must be relevant to the functions they perform. To cite but a crude example, to explain the difference in reactions that people will have to the two sentences 'dog bites man' and 'man bites dog', it is not enough just to talk about their representations or ideas of 'man', 'bites', and 'dog'. One must also postulate representations of the relations among these ideas and this representation of their relations must play some role in explaining these differences. There must then be something that is capable of noticing these differences in structure and then acting accordingly. This is a very old problem that associationist psychologists left unanswered and at least some philosophers attempted to solve through postulating mysterious mental faculties or powers. Durkheim is also weak on this problem and in the same way as the associationists. When he tried to explain how collective representations interact with each other and with individual representations, he would appeal to such things as the 'fusion' of representations, social forces, or collective effervescence, but never to any social process that involved the very structure of representations. Regarding these representations as taking on a life of their own and requiring no conscious mind to interpret them, Durkheim gives the impression that he is unconcerned with the meanings of social facts.

Crépeau proposes that the social sciences would be better off without the notion of collective representations, at least as it has come down to us through the tradition of Durkheim, Mauss, Lévi-Strauss, and Descola [Crépeau]. Within this tradition, concepts such as representation, category, framework, and structure have been used to separate the mind from the world. Crépeau draws on recent work in philosophy to argue that it is time for anthropology to stop thinking of language and concepts as some sort of veil between us and nature, but rather as a means to express relations among things that is very much a part of nature.

Bloor attempts to carry out something like Crépeau's project through his re-interpretation of collective representations as social institutions [Bloor]. He removes meaning and hence truth from inside the head and relocates it in relations among people and things in society. Thus he helps us get at least part of the way to the normative nature of meaning and knowledge claims. However, given Durkheim's defense of the correspondence theory of truth in his lectures on pragmatism, Bloor's re-interpretation is more along the lines of what Durkheim should have said than what he did say. Also, it is not clear why Bloor wants to hold on to the term 'collective representations' or how what he calls their self-referential character is supposed to work. There is no problem with his notion that the *object* of collective representations or social institutions is the institution or representation itself. However, it is difficult to understanding his claim that the institution or representation is also the *subject* of these representations. To 'represent' literally means 'to present again'. Hence, for something to be a *representation*, there must be something to which it is *present*. It is not clear to what a representation could be present if not a conscious mind. At least, as I argued above, there must be something that is capable of acting on representations in accordance with their structures.

Crépeau and Bloor alike stand opposed to Rawls's call for a return to foundationalism, epistemological givens, and a representational notion of truth. The danger is that in giving these things up they may lead us back to the conceptual relativism that Rawls and I would avoid. Perhaps the Darwinian ecology of knowledge that Crépeau suggests may be the way to avoid relativism and yet maintain the social character of knowledge. That is, the way to connect our knowledge up with reality and thus to justify it may not be to seek foundations in its socially variable causes, but rather to consider the social functions of our concepts and how they help us to adapt. What is needed is some functional, adaptationist account of how human beings as social, linguistic agents evolved. Such an account is needed to explain both the fact that there are universally shared ways of thinking that appear to be necessary for social life and the fact that there are important local and even individual variations in these universally shared concepts.

References

Alexander, J. (1982) *Theoretical Logic in Sociology*, Berkeley, Cal.: University of California Press.

Alpert, H. (1961) *Emile Durkheim and his Sociology*, New York: Russell & Russell.

Bloor, D. (1982) 'Durkheim and Mauss Revisited: Classification and the Sociology of Knowledge', *Studies in History and Philosophy of Science* 13(4):267–97.

Bloor, D. (1999) 'Collective Representations as Social Institutions', in W. S. F. Pickering (ed.), *Durkheim and Representation*, London: Routledge.

Boudon, R. (1995) 'Weber and Durkheim: Beyond the Differences a Common Important Paradigm?', *Revue internationale de philosophie* 49 (192):221–39.

Brooks, J. (1996) 'The Definition of Sociology and the Sociology of Definition: Durkheim's *Rules of Sociological Method* and High School

Philosophy in France', *Journal of the History of the Behavioral Sciences* 32 (4):379–407.

Brooks, J. (1998) *The Eclectic Legacy*, Newark, Del.: University of Delaware Press.

Crépeau, R. (1996) 'Une Ecologie de la connaissance est-elle possible?', *Anthropologie et Sociétés*, 20 (3):15–32.

Dennes, W. (1924) 'The Methods and Presuppositions of Group Psychology', *University of California Publications in Philosophy* 6(1):1–182.

Douglas, J. (1967) *The Social Meanings of Suicide*, Princeton, NJ: Princeton University Press.

Durkheim, E. (1887a) 'La Philosophie dans les universités allemandes', *Revue internationale de l'enseignement* 13:313–38, 423–40.

— (1895a) *Les Règles de la méthode sociologique*, Paris: Alcan.

— (1901c) 2nd. edn, Paris: Alcan.

— (t.1982) by W. D. Halls, *The Rules of Sociological Method and Selected Texts on Sociology and its Method*, New York: Free Press.

— (1897a) *Le Suicide: étude de sociologie*, Paris: Alcan.

— (t.1951) by J. Spaulding and G. Simpson, *Suicide: A Study in Sociology*, New York: Free Press.

— (1903a(i)) (with Marcel Mauss) 'De quelque formes primitives de classification: contribution à l'étude des représentations collectives', *L'Année sociologique* VI:1–72.

— (t.1963b) by R. Needham, *Primitive Classification*, Chicago: University of Chicago Press.

— (1912a) *Les Formes élémentaires de la vie religieuse*, Paris: Alcan.

— (t.1995c) by Karen Fields, *The Elementary Forms of Religious Life*, New York: Free Press.

— (1996a) *Cours de philosophie fait au Lycée de Sens*. Written student lecture notes taken by André Lalande in Durkheim's philosophy course in 1883–4. Bibliothèque de la Sorbonne, manuscript number 2351. Also available on microfilm from the University of Wisconsin, Madison, Microforms Center, film number 9307, and at http://www.relst.uiuc.edu/durkheim/Texts/1884a/00.html.

Gane, M. (1988) *On Durkheim's Rules of Sociological Method*, London: Routledge.

Gehlke, C. (1915) *Emile Durkheim's Contribution to Sociological Theory*, New York: AMS Press.

Gieryn, T. (1982) 'Durkheim's Sociology of Scientific Knowledge', *Journal of the History of the Behavioral Sciences* 28:107–29.

Godlove, T. (1986) 'Epistemology in Durkheim's *Elementary Forms of the Religious Life*', *Journal of the History of Philosophy* 24(3):385–401.

Godlove, T. (1989) *Religion, Interpretation, and Diversity of Belief: the Framework Model from Kant to Durkheim and Davidson*, New York: Cambridge University Press.

Goldenweiser, A. (1915) 'Review of Durkheim, Emile, *Les Formes Elementaires de la Vie Religieuse*', *American Anthropologist* **17**:719–35.

Gross, N. (1997) 'Durkheim's Pragmatism Lectures: A Contextual Interpretation', *Sociological Theory* 15(2):126–49.

Hirst, P. (1975) *Durkheim, Bernard, and Epistemology*, London: Routledge and Kegan Paul.

Hume, D. (1966) *Enquiries Concerning the Human Understanding and Concerning the Principles of Morals* (1st published 1748), Oxford: Clarendon Press.

Johnson, T., Dandeker, C. and Ashworth, C. (1984) *The Structure of Social Theory*, Basingstoke, UK: Macmillan.

Jones, R. (1994) 'Ambivalent Cartesians: Durkheim, Montesquieu, and Method', *American Journal of Sociology* 100 (1):1–39.

Jones, R. (1996) 'Durkheim, Realism, and Rousseau', *Journal of the History of the Behavioral Sciences* 32(4):330–53.

Laudan, L. (1990) *Science and Relativism*, Chicago: University of Chicago Press.

Lukes, S. (1973) *Emile Durkheim: His Life and Work*, New York: Penguin Books.

Lukes, S. (1982) 'Introduction' to *The Rules of Sociological Method and Selected Texts on Sociology and its Method*, trans. by W. D. Halls, New York: Free Press.

Parsons, T. (1937) *The Structure of Social Action*, New York: Free Press.

Rawls, A. (1996) 'Durkheim's Epistemology: The Neglected Argument', *American Journal of Sociology* 102(2):430–82.

Rawls, A. (1997) 'Durkheim's Epistemology: The Initial Critique, 1915–1924', *The Sociological Quarterly* 38(1):111–45.

Rawls, A. (1998) 'Durkheim's Challenge to Philosophy: Human Reason Explained as a Product of Enacted Social Practice', *American Journal of Sociology* 104(3):861–75.

Schaub, E. (1920) 'A Sociological Theory of Knowledge', *Philosophical Review* 29:319–39.

Schmaus, W. (1994) *Durkheim's Philosophy of Science and the Sociology of Knowledge: creating an intellectual niche*, Chicago: University of Chicago Press.

Schmaus, W. (1995) 'Explanation and Essence in *The Rules of Sociological Method* and *The Division of Labor in Society*', *Sociological Perspectives* 38(1):57–75.

Schmaus, W. (1998) 'Rawls, Durkheim, and Causality', *American Journal of Sociology* 104(3):846–60.

Schmaus, W. (2000a) 'Representations in Durkheim's Sens lectures: an early approach to the subject', in W. S. F. Pickering (ed.), *Durkheim and Representation*, London: Routledge.

Schmaus, W. (2000b) 'Meaning and Representation in the Social Sciences', in W. S. F. Pickering (ed.), *Durkheim and Representation*, London: Routledge.

Taylor, S. (1982) *Durkheim and the Study of Suicide*, New York: St. Martin's Press.

Wallwork, E. (1972) *Durkheim: Morality and Milieu*, Cambridge, Mass: Harvard University Press.

Watts Miller, W. (1993) 'Durkheim's Montesquieu', *British Journal of Sociology* 44(4):692–712.

Watts Miller, W. (1996) *Durkheim, Morals and Modernity*, London: UCL Press.

Selected Items

Bloor, D. (2000) 'Collective representations as social institutions', in W. S. F. Pickering (ed.), *Durkheim and Representations*, London: Routledge, pp. 157–76.

Brooks, J, I., III (1996) 'The definition of sociology and the sociology of definition: Durkheim's *Rules of Sociological Method* and high school philosophy in France', *Journal of the History of the BehavioralSciences* 33(4):379–407.

Crépeau, R. (1996) 'Une écologie de la connaissance est-elle possible?', *Anthropologie et sociétés* 20(3):15–32.

Gross, N. (1997) 'Durkheim's pragmatism lectures: a contextual interpretation', *Sociological Theory* 15(2):126–49.

Jones, R. A. (1994) 'Ambivalent cartesians: Durkheim, Montesquieu, and Method', *American Journal of Sociology* 100(1):1–39.

Rawls, A. (1996) 'Durkheim's epistemology: the neglected argument', *American Journal of Sociology* 102(2):430–82.

Rawls, A. (1998) 'Durkheim's challenge to philosophy: human reason explained as a product of enacted social practice', *American Journal of Sociology* 104(3):887–901.

Schmaus, W. (1998) 'Rawls, Durkheim and causality: a critical discussion', *American Journal of Sociology* 104(3):872–86.

Schmaus, W. (2000) 'Meaning and representation in the social sciences', in W. S. F. Pickering (ed.), *Durkheim and Representations*, London: Routledge, pp. 139–56.

Watts Miller, W. (1996) 'Towards a new spirit of the laws', in W. Watts Miller, *Durkheim, Morals and Modernity*, London: UCL Press, pp. 47–71.

Chapter 5

Morality and ethics

W. Watts Miller

Durkheim's work on morality is complex, many sided and an integral part of his work as a whole. It is open to a number of interpretations, has roots in a spread of influences and can be taken up and developed in a variety of ways. Trying to put together an overall account is a formidable task, even with the space available in a book (or at least this was so in writing *Durkheim, Morals and Modernity* (Watts Miller 1996)). Yet it is important that there are attempts at a general picture, especially within the limits and economy of an article. An essay by Isambert sets out to do this and so provides an entry into the topic of morality [Isambert 1993a]. At the same time his sketch of Durkheim's moral theory is better appreciated after re-reading more specialist contributions. These include one of his own, and they divide, very roughly, into three groups. The first centres round a key text, Durkheim's *Moral Education* (1925a). The next explores issues to do with the individual, society and a 'cult of man'. The final group explores modern ills as well as modern ideals, and so whether or not there is much room for hope nowadays.

Moral education

The lecture-course on moral education was probably first given, not in 1902–3 as suggested by its editor, Fauconnet, but in 1898–9 (Besnard 1993a, Watts Miller 1997). Moreover, it is not just about moral education. Part One is in fact the main written-up text by Durkheim on ethics. It identifies three core elements of moral life, discussed as 'the spirit of discipline', 'attachment to groups' and 'autonomy of the will'. It is Part Two that focuses on moral education. It begins with lectures on teaching the spirit of discipline. It next has lectures on teaching attachment to groups. It then just stops, without any on teaching autonomy. There is reason to suspect that the text is incomplete, and that key lectures on an education for autonomy have been lost. This undermines the criticism of Durkheim's supposed silence on such an education as 'un blanc significatif' (Filloux 1997:95).

Doubts are also possible about Isambert's sketch of Durkheim's 'sociology of moral facts' [Isambert 1993a]. Just as *The Elementary Forms* (Durkheim 1912a) looks for universal elements of religious life, so *Moral Education* sees attachment and the spirit of discipline as universal elements of moral life. And in both texts the appeal to universals involves a critique of contemporary malaise. The strategy was not new. *The Division of Labour* (Durkheim 1893b), also in a concern for modern malaise, appeals to solidarity as a universal element of moral life, indeed as its very source. The division of labour is moral, therefore, if it is a force for solidarity (see Chapter 8 here). And it needs to be the solidarity, not merely of negative, dutiful respect, but of positive fellow-feeling and attachment. Yet Isambert contrasts an 'early' Durkheim, who emphasizes the constraints of obligatoriness, with a 'late' Durkheim who also emphasizes the moral emotions of attachment and who insists on a dualism of duty and the good. And the quite late Durkheim is seen in 'The determination of moral facts', a discussion paper of 1906 (1906b). But these two sides of morality are to be found all through his work. It is nearer the truth to see a development in his ethics of theorization about their nature and relationship. The development was well under way in the moral education lectures of 1898–9 and continued in the paper of 1906, just mentioned.

Durkheim's views on moral education, especially his concern with teaching children discipline and respect for authority, were famously criticized by Piaget (1977). This was so because of a concern for the solidarity and attachments of the peer group.

Through practices such as the game of marbles, children can themselves grow into a deeper, more co-operative as well as more autonomous sense of morality. In sympathizing less with Durkheim and more with Tolstoy and his ideal of the school as a practice fostering co-operation and autonomy, Filloux is on the same general side (Filloux 1997). An article by Turner partly brackets this debate [Turner]. In a way all these writers are on the same side but from a very different position. It rests on an assumption which Turner sees as entrenched in modern ethics and which he characterizes as 'justificationalism'. It is all about deducing moral judgements from a chain of reasons that end in a highly abstract, supreme and overriding principle. The importance of the article is not just that it defends Durkheim against attacks by Kohlberg, one of the most influential modern American writers on moral education, as well as against the views of Gilligan, his ex-student, critic and one of a group of very important writers on feminist ethics. It is that they are so opposed to Durkheim in their approaches, which express the same thing, a basic justificationalism. Even if Kohlberg is weak on moral emotion and tends to appeal to a masculine-rationalist ethic of justice while Gilligan appeals to a feminist ethic of care and attachment, both appeal to justice as a supreme principle or to attachment as a supreme principle. It is not an appeal to them as virtues, embedded in the experiences, practices and, Turner emphasizes, rituals of social life.

It is this approach to ethics that he defends and sees in Durkheim. My own article also defends it, if in a perhaps too abstract way, but focusing on other aspects of Durkheim's concern with 'the complexity of things' [Watts Miller 1998]. This includes trying to identify a cluster of virtues at work in 'the spirit of discipline', another set at work in 'attachment', and what they might all have to do with an emerging autonomy. It also includes an attempt to rescue autonomy from its oversimple, over-individualistic interpretation evident nowadays, and to re-link it to the complexities, in Kant as well as Durkheim, of the individual as a person in an organic union of persons.

A particular problem, here, is helped by a return to Turner's interest in rituals. An example is Durkheim's discussion paper of 1906 and how it was presented, queried and debated, with the hope of persuading by argument but without expectation of agreement (nor was there any) (Durkheim 1906b). What is going on in this 'ritual' – a familiar one – of a liberal public culture? It does not seem to me adequate just to see it as embedding norms of 'tolerance'. It requires something more, a sense of 'delicacy', as Durkheim himself put it at one point in the discussion. This is a virtue that might be learnt readily in practice, yet is difficult to formulate and theorize. On the contrary, a risk is an unholy alliance in which authoritarian and lumpen-relativist positions share the same assumption, that claim objectivity and accept disagreement. A liberal public culture involves commitment to some sort of objective discourse and the hope of arriving at agreement, if only, perhaps, in a Habermasian ideal speech situation. At the same time it involves acceptance of such an ideal as unrealizable – indeed, as somehow fundamentally misguided – and it has an expectation of a continuing, legitimate diversity of views. Put in other terms, it is about us as individual personalities – that is, not just as individuals, content with the expression of our own different, subjective opinions, yet not just as persons, able to debate our way on everything to a same shared understanding.

The individual, society and a 'cult of man'

Issues to do with the individual, the person, society and a 'cult of man' are a minefield. They are explored in the next group of articles. Isambert puts a basic worry very well [Isambert 1993b]. Durkheim undertook a difficult, risk-strewn search to do two things. One was to try to establish the pre-eminence of society. The other was to try to provide the individual, in this way, with strong, vigorous roots. Yet did he destroy these, with all his stress on 'society'? Or again, even if his vision of the developing and flourishing individual-in-society is a coherent ideal, he himself recognized how social forces can harm, oppress and indeed kill off individuals. In the world, nowadays, is this not the pre-eminent 'social fact'?

Of course, part of the minefield is that 'the individual' has many meanings in Durkheim's work. But so has 'society'. If it is sometimes a Supreme Being, it is also a catch-all reference to any form, aspect or process of social and collective life. Isambert, however, is especially concerned with meanings of 'the individual'. He mentions the individual human creature or 'organism'. But he passes on to concentrate on the individual of individuality and a particular, different and distinct character of one's own. This is certainly of crucial importance for Durkheim throughout his work, not least in his attacks on ideas of the individual as a self-sufficient, separate atom. More positively, it is a route to distinct yet interdependent and attached individuals, and so to social cohesion. But individuality is also a route, in part via solidarity, to developing and flourishing as persons. It is axiomatic, for Durkheim, that this is impossible for the individual as atom. Indeed it is in generating such egoistic or anomic currents of thinking, feeling and acting that the modern social world can be a force that harms and kills us. Here, however, it seems necessary to bring the individual flesh-and-blood human back in. If anyone is at risk, it is this individual – but who also stands to benefit, given Durkheim's neo-Aristotelian ideas, from society as a transformative force that unlocks energies within human-nature-as-potentiality, as a waiting-to-be-developed-power-to-flourish. In any case, and as Isambert brings out, Durkheim goes beyond the distinct, empirical (even if socially developed) individual to invoke the person. One reason is that regard for each of us as different individuals requires regard for everyone as a person, with the same status and dignity. But it is also to look, in modern individualism, for something that transcends us as individuals – a force that can command respect but also inspire us and mobilize ideals, and that is a common faith.

This leads on to Durkheim's insistence on the person as a modern centre of the sacred, and to his idea of a 'cult of man' (see Chapter 3 here). Pickering is perhaps the main recent critic of the idea [Pickering]. Cladis [1992] is one of the main supporters of its resort to the sacred, which is also defended, for example, by Thompson (1993). What are the fundamental lines of disagreement?

One of them has its source in an ambivalence in Durkheim himself. The idea of a cult of man, complete with symbols, rites, temples and priests, was not only not new, but its various expressions during as well as after the French Revolution had become both an object of ridicule and a source of embarrassment to Durkheim's republican contemporaries. In 'Individualism and the intellectuals', published in 1898 during the Dreyfus Affair, he went out of his way to distance himself from the idea of a cult that involved all the paraphernalia and 'external apparatus' of traditional religion (Durkheim 1898c). He insisted, instead, on keeping only to religion's essential core, 'a system of collective beliefs and practices that have a special authority'. But although, in *The Elementary Forms*, what is eternal in religion might at first sight appear the same – faith and the cult – it is in a context that, amongst other things, includes approving references to the Revolution's rites and festivals, worry about a lack of such things in a contemporary 'moral mediocrity', and emphasis on the dependence of social life on a 'vast symbolism'. There seems a return, in other words, to the idea of a 'cult of man' complete with an external apparatus and all.

Pickering does not see much if any evidence of such a cult nowadays, argues that the appeal to religious language was and remains divisive and, though happy to go along with support for human rights through beliefs and practices 'with a special authority', is unhappy with counting this a manifestation of the sacred. Cladis' strength, with which Pickering might agree, is his emphasis on core conviction, belief and commitment – and so on something more than the 'ethical principles' of philosophy books – but also on how such shared conviction, which liberals need as much as anyone, can still let in liberal room for conflict and pluralism. Yet does any of this take us to the realm of the sacred – as analysed in Durkheim's writings taken overall? It is necessary to ask how it works out in terms of his ideas of the sacred as incommensurable, plural and transcendent (but also immanent). And it is necessary to ask about its symbols and rites, given their re-appearance in *The Elementary Forms*.

Pickering might draw support on this front from the recent massive work of Nora and his collaborators on *lieux de mémoire*. These, with all their symbolism and ceremony, are described as nowadays little more than 'vestiges' and 'fleeting incursions of the sacred', 'the rituals of a ritual-less society' (Nora 1996:7). On the other hand, Cladis might draw support from the work of Maffesoli, who looks elsewhere for the energies of the sacred and sees a 'veritable re-enchantment' of the world (Maffesoli 1996:28). Or is this view too sunny and optimistic?

Modern ills and modern ideals: what might we hope?

Isambert sees Durkheim as very much against ideas of a basic, irreconcilable opposition between the individual and society [Ismabert 1993b]. So does Cladis, at least in the piece just discussed. This article includes a detailed analysis of 'The dualism of human nature', an article of 1913 which features *homo duplex*, and which is sometimes cited as evidence of Durkheim's belief, in fact, in a radical conflict between individual and social man (Durkheim 1913b). As well as arguing against this interpretation of the article, Cladis stresses how it does not fit in with Durkheim's views in his work as a whole. He also stresses how, if Durkheim often seems to set up dualisms, it is to go on to leave behind and transcend them. Isambert points out how it happens in the case of the dualism of duty and the good. Moreover, this general strategy, in which Durkheim again and again negotiated his way to a position that was 'either a middle way between opposite extremes or a synthesis of the partial truths of other approaches', is the focus of a recent study by Brooks (1998:228). So farewell to *homo duplex*?

Apparently not. He (or she) continues to crop up, as in the article by Shilling and Mellor, but also in another article by Cladis, who, in a paragraph at the end, retreats from his earlier, carefully laid out views [Shilling and Mellor; Cladis 1996].

In his article, Cladis discusses Rousseau and Durkheim on human nature and asks the question (made famous by Kant) – what can we hope for? It involves an original and illuminating exploration of Rousseau himself. It also goes into Durkheim's lectures on Rousseau, which include an attack on him for setting up a dualism of human nature and a radical conflict between the individual and society (Durkheim 1918b). The lectures, by the way, can be dated to around or just after 1896. They make much of a 'remarkable passage' that in fact is from a manuscript of *The Social Contract*, was omitted from the original and subsequent published editions, and did not become generally available in France until a new critical edition of that year (Watts Miller 1998:135). But let us get back to Cladis, his exposition of twists and turns, inconsistencies and ambivalences in Durkheim's criticism of Rousseau, and his thought that Durkheim increasingly came to share Rousseau's gloom. Why? Because of a shift, culminating in the 1913 article, towards acceptance of a radical conflict between individual and social man (Durkheim 1913b). Whether or not true, does the interpretation open out lines of theoretical enquiry worth taking up?

Cladis stresses that for Rousseau, with the individual's entrance into society, 'the basic conditions of goodness and happiness… are also the conditions of inequality, hypocrisy, greed and cruelty'. Then this is not about a radical conflict between man in the state of nature and man in society. It suggests a conflict built into man's waiting-to-be-developed social nature, and so also a conflict between different forces at work within a social world. That is, it links with Durkheim's internalist programme. This, in *Suicide*, roots modern ills in the same dynamic as modern ideals (Durkheim 1897a). Or, in the

1902 preface to *The Division of Labour*, it diagnoses a modern state of anomie amounting to a state of war and clutches at a hope against hope in tackling it.

Book III of *The Division of Labour* set up an ideal that produced a sense of depression amongst some of the Durkheimians, as noted by Besnard (1993b:197). My own attempt to rework it might make the ideal more coherent, but leaves it just as high-minded, and so might seem similarly improbable and depressing [Watts Miller 1996]. The point, however, is not just to say what a commonwealth of persons in which all of us can develop and flourish would look like. It is also to identify the main obstacles to this. They can be found, not in a radical conflict between the individual and society, but in conflicts between key ideals generated by our society, as well as in pathologies that are part of the very same dynamic as these ideals.

In any case it is at least as depressing, if not more so, to enter the grim world of the disciplinary society analysed in the work of Foucault. It is certainly a world of disenchantment, with no hint of the sacred, not even vestiges and fleeting incursions of it. It is described as a 'negative utopia' by Gephart (1999:59), and here by Ramp as 'the dark side of utopian dreams of citizenship, community and individual autonomy'. This is in the essay that comes after my own, and that contrasts with but also complements it. The actuality of 'the dark side' of a commonwealth of persons is part of this ideal itself and generated from within the same world. Indeed, after noting that one reading of Durkheim is that he is an advocate of just the sort of modernizing governmentality Foucault sought to expose, Ramp goes on to suggest the possibility of a more fertile dialogue between Durkheimian and Foucaultian approaches. One way is to explore a situation in which, in an anomic *society*, the agendas of its agencies and apparatuses are not about returning this to its normal state but are about returning deviant *individuals* to the discipline of self-surveillance and self-regulation on behalf of the authority placed in charge of them. This seems to me highly applicable to current trends throughout the schools, universities, hospitals, offices and other institutions of new Labour new Britain, in which spin about a 'third way' is part and parcel of a disciplinary, managerialist regime. But Ramp also goes on to suggest a basic Durkheimian-Foucaultian split here, to do with 'the death of god' and its Foucaultian aftermath, 'the death of the social'. What is at stake, the essay concludes, is a shift from the problematic of the individual-the social to that of the subject-the political and to a world of the 'radically contingent', in which things are no longer 'bathed in the growing light of an evolutionary dawn'.

The essay by Shilling and Mellor already referred to, offers a picture that is very different from all this – but that, again, both conflicts with and complements it [Shilling and Mellor]. They write from a Durkheimian perspective, to discuss and critique a whole range of contemporary social theorists. But in their search for collective ferment, sociality and the sacred, they are especially interested in Maffesoli and his vision, in *The Time of the Tribes*, of a veritable re-enchantment of the world. So it helps to say something, first, about Maffesoli himself.

An obvious yet often overlooked fact about the Australia of *The Elementary Forms* is that it does not have apparatuses such as the state. Maffesoli seems to me unerringly right to link the power of the sacred with the underground, bottom-up power (*puissance*) of sociality and collective ferment rather than with the organizing, top-down power (*pouvoir*) of institutions and managerialist bastilles. Of course, and as the article by Pickering points out, Durkheim had high idealistic hopes for the state. On the other hand, he also diagnosed a deep-rooted modern political malaise. His worries about the state nowadays find expression in a widespread disillusionment with it, shown also in the work not only of Foucault but also of Maffesoli. *The Time of the Tribes* has given up on hope for a republic of persons. Its hope is instead in a running underground battle in which the *puissance* of sociality continues to resist the *pouvoir* of institutions, and so in a power conflict where, if *puissance* never wins out, neither does *pouvoir*. This then is one of the most effective contemporary Durkheimian replies to Foucault. There *has been* a 'death of the social' – but for the same reason that there has been a 'death of the political'. The ideal of a society-*and*-republic of persons has lost its magic and mystique. There *is not* a 'death of the social' – but again for the same reason that there has been a 'death of the political'. The energies of sociality remain. The mystique of the republic has sunk deep into the mire of *pouvoir* and *politique*.

Shilling and Mellor criticize Maffesoli's 'optimism'. They are in a way mistaken, on the grounds just discussed. In another way they seem correct. The sacred unleashes divine but also demonic energies – as in Durkheim's remark that the Revolution's collective ferment transformed the ordinary individual, 'into hero or butcher'. Maffesoli underplays the demonic side, just as Mestrovic is criticized for overplaying it. One strength of the essay is to emphasize this divine-demonic ambivalence of the sacred. Another is to emphasize, like Maffesoli, the role of 'emotive community', not least in the transformative powers of effervescence.

This can apply even to Durkheim's interest in 'intellectual effervescence'. A good case of it is the Durkheimian group itself, with an 'intellectual exhilaration' in which they were 'perhaps almost delirious' (Mauss 1998:36). Here, however, another ambivalence running through Durkheim's work returns. Perhaps Shilling and Mellor overdo the Dionysian side of the sacred, just as others amongst us, in going on about a society, commonwealth or republic of persons, overdo the more rationalist and restrained, Apollonian side. Maybe, to try to capture the various ambivalences but also the state we are in now, we need to talk and think about 'tribes of persons'.

References

Besnard, P. (1993a) 'De la datation des cours pédagogiques de Durkheim à la recherche du thème dominant de son œuvre', in F. Cardi and J. Plantier (eds) *Durkheim, sociologue de l'éducation*, Paris: L'Harmattan.

Besnard, P. (1993b) 'Les pathologies des sociétés modernes', in P. Besnard, M. Borlandi and P. Vogt (eds) *Division du travail et lien social: la thèse de Durkheim un siècle après*, Paris: Presses Universitaires de France.

Brooks, J. I. (1998) *The Eclectic Legacy: Academic Philosophy and the Human Sciences in Nineteenth-Century France*, Newark: University of Delaware Press.

Durkheim, E. (1893b) *De la Division du travail social*, Paris: Alcan.

— (t.1984) by W. D. Halls, *The Division of Labour in Society*, London: Macmillan.

— (1897a) *Le Suicide: étude de sociologie*, Paris: Alcan.

— (t.1951) by J. A. Spaulding and G. Simpson, *Suicide: a study in sociology*, London: Routledge and Kegan Paul.

— (1898c) 'Individualisme et les intellectuels', *Revue bleue*, 4th series, X:7–13.

— (1906b) 'La Détermination du fait social', *Bulletin de la Société française de philosophie* VI:169–212.

— (1912a) *Les Formes élémentaires de la vie religieuse*, Paris: Alcan.

— (t.1995) by K. Fields, *The Elementary Forms of Religious Life*, New York: The Free Press.

— (1913b) Contribution to the discussion: 'Le Problème religieux et la dualité de la nature humaine', *Bulletin de la Société française de philosophie* XIII: 63–75, 80–7, 90–100, 108–11.

— (1918b) 'Le "Contrat social" de Rousseau', *Revue de métaphysique et de morale* XXV:1–23, 129–61.

— (1925a) *L'Education morale*, introduction by Paul Fauconnet, Paris: Alcan.

— (t.1961) by E. K. Wilson and H. Schnurer, *Moral Education*, New York: Free Press.

Filloux, J.-C. (1997) 'Durkheim critique de Tolstoï, ou d'un aveugle dans la sociologie durkheimienne', *Durkheimian Studies/Etudes durkheimiennes*, n.s. 3:83–95.

Gephart, W. (1999) 'The Realm of Normativity in Durkheim and Foucault', in M. S. Cladis (ed.) *Durkheim and Foucault: perspectives on education and punishment*, Oxford: Durkheim Press.

Maffesoli, M. (1996) *The Time of the Tribes*, London: Sage.

Mauss, M. (1998) 'An Intellectual Self-portrait', in W. James and N. J. Allen (eds) *Marcel Mauss: A Centenary Tribute*, New York and Oxford: Berghahn Books.

Nora, P. (ed.) (1996–98) *Realms of Memory*, 3 vols, New York: Columbia University Press.

Piaget, J. (1977) *The Moral Judgment of the Child*, London: Penguin. (1st edn 1932).

Thompson, K. (1993) 'Wedded to the Sacred', in W. S. F. Pickering and W. Watts Miller (eds) *Individualism and Human Rights in the Durkheimian Tradition*, Oxford: British Centre for Durkheimian Studies.

Watts Miller, W. (1996) *Durkheim, Morals and Modernity*, London: UCL Press.

Watts Miller, W. (1997) 'Durkheim's course on moral education: the issue of its date, and the lost lectures on autonomy', *Durkheimian Studies/Etudes durkheimiennes*, n.s. 3: 21–4.

Watts Miller, W. (1998) Review of W. Schmaus (ed.) *Durkheimian Sociology. Durkheimian Studies/Etudes durkheimiennes*, n.s., 4:130–6.

Selected Items

Cladis, M. S. (1992) 'The individual in society: a sacred marriage?', in M. S. Cladis, *A Communitarian Defense of Liberalism*, Stanford: Stanford University Press, pp. 115–35.

Cladis, M. S. (1996) 'What can we hope for? Rousseau and Durkheim on human nature', *Journal of the History of the Behavioral Sciences* 32(4), 456–72.

Isambert, F.-A. (1993a) 'Durkheim's sociology of moral facts', in S. Turner (ed.), *Emile Durkheim: Sociologist and Moralist*, London: Routledge, pp. 193–210.

Isambert, F.-A. (1993b) 'Durkheim et l'individualité', in W. S. F. Pickering and W. Watts Miller (eds), *Individualism and Human Rights*, Oxford: The British Centre for Durkheimian Studies, pp. 7–31.

Pickering, W. S. F. (1993) 'Human rights and the individual: an unholy alliance created by Durkheim?', in W. S. F. Pickering and W. Watts Miller (eds), *Individualism and Human Rights*, Oxford: The British Centre for Durkheimian Studies, pp. 51–76.

Ramp, W. (1999) 'Durkheim and Foucault on the genesis of the disciplinary society', in M. S. Cladis (ed.), *Durkheim and Foucault: Perspectives on Education and Punishment*, Oxford: Durkheim Press, pp. 71–103.

Shilling, C. and Mellor, P. (1998) 'Durkheim, morality and modernity: collective effervescence, homo duplex and the sources of moral action', *British Journal of Sociology* 49(2), 195–209.

Turner, S. P. (1998) 'Kohlberg's critique of Durkheim's Moral Education', in G. Walford and W. S. F. Pickering (eds), *Durkheim and Modern Education*, London: Routledge, pp. 46–58.

Watts Miller, W. (1996) 'Modern ills and modern ideals', in W. Watts Miller, *Durkheim, Morals and Modernity*, London: UCL Press, pp. 117–37.

Watts Miller, W. (1998) 'Teaching autonomy', in G. Walford and W. S. F. Pickering (eds), *Durkheim and Modern Education*, London: Routledge, pp. 72–91.

Chapter 6

Political sociology

Josep R. Llobera

As a result of the work of Giddens (1972) and Lacroix (1981), as well as that of others, it has become a well-known fact that neither in the writings of Durkheim nor in *L'Année sociologique* can we find a clear sociological category that can be labelled 'political sociology' or even politics. However, it is also true that Durkheim dealt with a number of topics that fall within what today would be called political sociology. It is also suggested that when dealing with political issues Durkheim's approach was more normative than sociological.

Why is there no place in Durkheim's writings for a political sociology? He was, of course, well aware that social scientists and political commentators often referred to political realities, but nonetheless he rejected the need of such a rubric. Favre has suggested three reasons for the suppression of the 'political' (1983:202–3):

1. Because political phenomena were gratuitous and contingent, and hence no social science could be created to explain them.

2. Because the 'political' was already dealt with by other disciplines in other university faculties (law, etc.).

3. Because after 1897 Durkheim gave primacy to his studies on religion and relegated other interests to obscurity.

In addition to Favre's points it is possible to say with Jean-Claude Filloux (1970) that many of the early writings of

Durkheim, from his first book reviews to his thesis on Montesquieu of 1892 (1892a), are clearly intended to criticize the 'political sciences' of his time, which he found mystifying and moralizing. In *Les Règles de la méthode sociologique* (1895a) he remarked that concepts such as the state, democracy, socialism, etc. – in a nutshell, political terms – were not sociologically sound because they were somewhat vague and imprecise. Furthermore, they were often used from a normative standpoint. Elsewhere he referred to them as 'those bastard speculations, half theoretical and half practical, half science and half art, which are sometimes still confused, but wrongly, with sociology' (Durkheim 1973a:42). Durkheim insisted that all political phenomena, whether they relate to the state or political ideas, had to be studied objectively. Most 'political scientists' were either men of action or political philosophers. However, in a course taught in the 1890s (Durkheim 1950a), he looked at the state both from a descriptive and a normative perspective. He insisted that the latter was not a reflection of his preferences but rather consisted of what he believed were the objective conditions of industrial societies.

While it is quite accurate then to state that Durkheim was not, unlike Weber, a political sociologist, most contemporary authors would agree that there is a political sociology in his work. For Durkheim, the political sphere is not something that can be spotted in primitive societies; in fact it only acquires its proper shape in modern societies, that is, in societies that exhibit a 'degree of complexity in social organization' (Giddens 1986:2). Durkheim, however, did not think that the state is a precondition for the existence of a political society. The state appears in the long evolutionary process that goes from societies characterized by mechanical solidarity to those characterized by organic solidarity.

Durkheim's conception of the state is substantially different from that of Weber. While the latter conceives the state in terms of power, power for Durkheim is only one of its dimensions. Territory, which for Weber is also important, is not central at all for Durkheim. In fact, for Durkheim the most important feature of the modern state is that of a harbinger of the rights of the individual.

We have already mentioned that in *L'Année sociologique* there is no section labelled 'political sociology', although the rubric 'political organization' appeared permanently after volume IV. Generally speaking, political topics occupied little place in the journal, with the consequence that many political studies were never reviewed or received only cursory attention. Marcel Mauss provided perhaps another explanation of why politics was not a favourite topic among the Durkheimians. Simply put, politics is an art, while sociology is a science. However, this does not quite explain why there should not have been a sociology of politics which examined how societies are administered. In the end, we can only conclude with Favre that Durkheim 'had a bias against constituting a political sociology and a tendency to reduce political phenomena to their legal expression' (1983:213).

Durkheim's political sociology is found not only in the most obviously political of his texts – *Montesquieu* (1892a), *Leçons de sociologie* (1950a), and *Le Socialisme* (1928a) – but also in a variety of other, often diverse publications, including short reviews in *L'Année sociologique* and in political discussions. In addition, such a classic as *Les Formes élémentaires* (1912a) was read in a totally different way (Lacroix 1981). The fact that many of these texts were published posthumously, has made it difficult for scholars to grasp the contours of Durkheim's contribution to a political science. Admittedly this would be different from Durkheim's own vision of what the political was. Rather than being a dimension of society, the 'political' was the social whole, or at least that is how Lacroix (ibid.:208) reads Durkheim's texts.

In the same vein Lacroix insists that according to Durkheim, sociology had yet to provide scientific concepts that could deal with the everyday political reality that people were familiar with. Terms like state, democracy, sovereignty, socialism, nationalism and many others were widely used, but were highly ambiguous and unscientific. The fact that political actors of different types, from voters to politicians, held conceptions more about their behaviour was more of a hindrance than a help, given the fact that they were emotionally involved. Men of action often err about the motivations for their political behaviour. They may be unaware of the social forces that shape their conduct.

Durkheim was equally scathing about the political classifications which philosophers and politicians have elaborated over the centuries. They may or may not be useful, but on the whole they tend to be superficial and inappropriate for sociology. The reason is simply that they put too much emphasis on the idea that political institutions are simply the results of human will and forget that they have a life of their own. In addition, political practitioners have their particular agendas as to what is best for society, politically speaking.

Durkheim's political sociology is articulated around the intersection of three master concepts: political society, state and authority. The task of elaborating a political sociology, although formulated earlier on in Durkheim's career in texts like *Montesquieu* (1892a) and *The Division of Labour* (1893b), would continue throughout his writings. The posthumously published *Leçons de sociologie* (1950a) is the book which best represents his endeavours, which he began in the 1890s and continued until death.

Socialism, as an eminently political phenomenon of his time, could not but interest Durkheim (Filloux 1977). But what is socialism and what social millieu generates it? As a collective representation, socialism is an ideal and it is oriented towards the reconstruction of society according to a plan. By placing the political squarely in the realm of collective representations, he subjects it to his classical scientific treatment. This in no way precludes Durkheim from understanding the active, dynamic dimension of socialism. Nonetheless, at this stage in his intellectual evolution, Durkheim's concept of the political is still quite limited; it deals with the emergence of new ideas but has little to say about the state and forms of government.

In conclusion, if Durkheim had no explicit political sociology, then his ideas on this topic have to be elicited by interrogating a variety of his texts that have hitherto been envisaged in a different light. In fact, from the early 1970s onwards there has been a growing, though still small, literature on Durkheim and politics, covering topics such as the state, political legitimation, democracy and absolutism, socialism, nationalism, liberalism, fascism and so on.

The articles and texts selected for this field try to be representative of what has been written on Durkheim and politics in the 1990s, though one of the contributions is from the 1980s. It must be said that the number of chapters and articles available on the topic of Durkheim and politics is rather small in this period: there are at the most about 30 items on our topic for the period under consideration.

It is appropriate to start the selection of papers on Durkheim's political sociology with Vogt's article. It places Durkheim's sociology, particularly the study of morality, in the social, political, and academic framework of the Third Republic, and it shows its greatness, as well as its servitudes. Vogt examines Durkheim's political commitments, his support for the moderate left of his time, his academic politics and his establishment-based theories of education. In the final resort, however, Vogt walks the tightrope of defending the thesis that in his sociology Durkheim was both scientific and political. Many critics of the social sciences maintain that objectivity is not achievable because of the political dimension of these disciplines, which lead unavoidably to one type of bias or the other.

In his article, Lacroix maintains that Durkheim's approach to the society of his time is essentially political. This can be demonstrated by reference to the fact that his early intellectual concerns (in the form of book reviews) were on political texts; even more so, the original topic of his doctoral dissertation was centred on the problem of making individualism compatible

with socialism. Durkheim was firmly committed to understanding the French political horizon of his time and to that end he
examined the social framework in which it appeared, as well as
the antecedents that created it. Lacroix is keen to emphasize
that in addition to the structural-functionalist and objectivist
Durkheim there is also an action-oriented one.

Müller's text is an attempt to provide a general overview of
Durkheim's political sociology. According to him, Durkheim set
himself the task of solving three major questions that plagued
the Third Republic: how to achieve national legitimacy, how to
create a more egalitarian social order and how to produce democratic citizens through the educational system. In modern
society it is the division of labour that creates social solidarity
and at the same time constitutes the foundation of the moral
order. However, anomic situations are not unusual in modern
societies. The issue is whether the system can be self-regulatory
and self-correcting or whether, as Marx assumed, a revolution is
required to supersede the contradictions between capital and
labour. Durkheim is confident that industrial society can create
a new moral order.

Müller contends that neither in the *Division du travail social*
nor in *Leçons de sociologie* did Durkheim provide a satisfactory
account of three major issues: the role of collective actors, the
role of the state and the role of modern collective conscience.
Central to the development of the modern cult of the individual, is the emergence of what Müller calls a 'balance of power
between the professional groups and the democratic state'.
Durkheim believed that his programme of corporativism would
reconcile individualism and socialism. The accusation of collu-
sion with Mussolini's Fascism can be easily dismissed because
Durkheim never envisaged a totalitarian state, but rather an
institution which was autonomous and respected individual
freedoms.

With hindsight it is possible to assert that Durkheim was
better than Marx or Weber at grasping the future of modern
industrial society. Neither socialism nor bureaucratic rigidity

was triumphant at the end of the twentieth century, but rather a kind of reformism centered on what Müller calls 'regulated economies, modern welfare states and individualistic morality'.

The last general article is that of Bach. The author's main purpose is to show that political legitimation is one of the central concepts of Durkheim's political sociology [Bach]. In modern conditions, under important structural changes, political institutions may lose their legitimacy. One of Durkheim's key concerns is how to erect a new basis for legitimacy, both at the level of values and of institutions. Now, the modern national state has to come to terms with the issue of moral individualism which has developed in modern society. In fact, the national state emerged as an institution to answer problems of war and peace and it is not the appropriate institutional framework to foster moral individualism. There is consequently a loss of legitimacy.

It is obvious that a new idea of the state is required – an institution that makes possible the flourishing of the individual. This can only be achieved if the state embodies through its organizations the reality of individual rights and freedoms. It is the sacralization of the individual that will solve the problems of political legitimation in modern industrial society. Traditional religion may no longer be relevant for our times, but the 'religion of humanity' is its modern functional equivalent. Only a strong state can guarantee the rights of the individual, but to make sure that state does not become oppressive, occupational corporations are required to counterbalance its power.

Hearn's text finds Durkheim's corporatism an idea appropriate to conditions of advanced capitalism. He emphasizes that Durkheim's solution to a time of crisis is within the framework of a vigorous commitment to democracy, which distinguishes him from the more authoritarian approaches of the past (Saint-Simon, Comte), not to speak of the Mussolini's Fascists. Hearn, however, is dubious that corporatism, as it has developed in the Western world, has created a more active and democratic participation of citizens. For one thing, there are only three major actors at stake (the state, business organizations and labour associations); other societal groups have limited representation.

Hawkins looks at Durkheim's political thought through the ideas on citizenship. Durkheim adhered to the ideals of the Third Republic, including the idea of a secular, interventionist state, but was also a staunch defender of individual liberties. Durkheim had doubts, however, about popular sovereignty in so far as he was not sure that the masses knew where public interest lay – so complex and diversified was modern society and so specialized were individuals.

Durkheim's definition of the state in *Leçons de sociologie* was of a deliberative organ that is different and superior to other societal groups; the state through its legislative and executive organs acts on behalf of society as a whole. According to Hawkins, this definition excludes any reference to popular sovereignty. People are excluded from decision making. What modern society requires is not classical parliamentarism but the creation of elected professional bodies that can send representatives to the state organs. Voting is certainly not something that Durkheim valued positively; in fact, he believed that would probably fade away in the future. On the other hand, the collective effervescence that he had referred to in the *Les Formes élémentaires* could be extremely creative.

Llobera's text presents in some detail Durkheim's intervention in a number of areas that have to do with nationalism. It examines certain lesser known materials (public discussions, war writings, etc.) in which Durkheim develops some of his ideas on the subject-matter of nationalism. If it can be safely stated that there is no explicit theory of nationalism in Durkheim's corpus, it must be said that there is an implicit theory of nationalism in his *Les Formes élémentaires* and other texts. The chapter also emphasizes the role of Durkheim as a nation-builder in the context of the French Third Republic. Finally, although he generally thinks in terms of a political conception of the nation, in the course of his life he came to recognize the important role played by cultural and ethnic factors in the shaping of nations. Durkheim is well aware that the modern form of the nation is the result of a long evolution, and he sees reasons to think that it will continue to evolve to ever more complex and comprehensive forms.

Roth's article looks at the issue of gender and politics. There is little doubt that Durkheim was imbued, in many ways, by the ideals of the Enlightenment; he also upheld the principles of the French Revolution (freedom, equality and fraternity). However, and as it is well-known, Durkheim's universalism was marred by his exclusion of women. In fact, he maintained that the development of men and women went in separate ways and that gender equality was not part of the project of modernity. Roth emphasizes that Durkheim had to use, against his own methodological rules, a biological argument to maintain the social differentiation of men and women, which made them interdependent in the context of the nuclear family.

The final two items by Schwartz and Tiryakian put, so to speak, Durkheim's political sociology into practice. Schwartz's article is an attempt to bring Durkheim to bear with a specific historical reality: the assassination of President Lincoln in 1865. This crime provoked an indescribable state of effervescence which was obvious in the rituals of the funeral journey and in the official funeral itself. These events happened in spite of the fact that Lincoln was a controversial President. The article shows how he became sacralized through the power of ritual which created solidarity where before it was often lacking. With Lincoln's tragic, sacrificial death, the American people, who might have disliked him while alive, identified him with the nation and paid him the highest honours.

Tiryakian is convinced that Durkheim has more than an antiquarian interest and that is why he applies his concepts to the study of contemporary realities. He believes that Durkheim's collective effervescence and Weber's charisma are, if not all we need to account for the revolutions of 1989 in Central Europe, at least crucial concepts to grasp the final episodes of these events. It is precisely because these events involved massive participation of individuals in gatherings, demonstrations, public rituals, etc., that the ideas of collective effervescence and charisma are clearly relevant. Tiryakian notes that the coming together of people in public spaces often involved manipulation of religious symbols or its modern functional equivalents.

References

Durkheim, E. (1892a) *Quid Secundatus Politicae Scientiae Instituendae Contulerit*, Bordeaux: Gounouilhou.

— (1893b) *De la Division du travail social: étude sur l'organisation des sociétiés supérieures*, Paris: Alcan.

— (1895a) *Les Règles de la méthode sociologique*, Paris: Alcan.

— (1912a) *Les Formes élémentaires de la vie religieuse: le système totémique en Australie*, Paris: Alcan.

— (1928a) *Le Socialisme*, Paris: Alcan.

— (1950a) *Leçons de sociologie: physique des moeurs et du droit*, Istanbul: L'Université d'Istanbul. Paris: Presses Universitaires de France.

— (1973a) *Emile Durkheim on Morality and Society*. Selected Writings, R. B. Bellah (ed.), Chicago: University of Chicago Press.

Favre, P. (1983) 'The Absence of Political Sociology in the Durkheimian Classifications of the Social Sciences', in P. Besnard (ed.) *The Sociological Domain*, Cambridge: Cambridge University Press.

Filloux, J.-C. (1970) 'Introduction' to *La Science sociale et l'action* par E. Durkheim, Paris: Presses Universitaires de France.

Filloux, J.-C. (1977) *Durkheim et le socialisme*, Geneva: Droz.

Giddens, A. (1972) 'Durkheim's Political Sociology', *The Sociological Review* 20:477–519.

Giddens, A. (1986) 'Introduction' to A. Giddens (ed.), *Durkheim on Politics and the State*, Stanford, Cal.: Stanford University Press.

Lacroix, B. (1981) *Durkheim et le politique*, Montréal: Presses de l'Université de Montréal.

Selected Items

Bach, M. (1990) 'Individualism and legitimation: paradoxes and perspectives on the political sociology of Emile Durkheim', *Archives européenes de sociologie* XXXI:187–98.

Hawkins, M. (1995) 'Durkheim and republican citizenship', in K. Thompson (ed.), *Durkheim, Europe and Democracy*, Oxford: British Centre for Durkheimian Studies.

Hearn, F. (1985) 'Durkheim's political sociology: corporatism, state autonomy, and democracy', *Social Research* 52(1):151–77.

Lacroix, B. (1990) 'Aux origines des sciences sociales françaises: politique, société et temporalité dans l'oeuvre d'Emile Durkheim', *Archives de sciences sociales des religions* 69:109–27.

Llobera, J. R. (1994) 'Durkheim and the national question', in W. S. F. Pickering and H. Martins (eds), *Debating Durkheim*, London: Routledge.

Müller, H.-P. (1993) 'Durkheim's political sociology', in S. Turner (ed.), *Emile Durkheim Sociologist and Moralist*, London: Routledge.

Roth, G. (1990) 'Durkheim and the principles of 1789: the issue of gender equality', *Telos* 82:71–88.

Schwartz, B. (1991) 'Mourning and the making of a sacred symbol: Durkheim and the Lincoln assassination', *Social Forces* 70(2):343–64.

Tiryakian, E. A. (1995) 'Collective effervescence, social change and charisma: Durkheim, Weber and 1989', *International Sociology* 10(3):269–81.

Vogt, W. P. (1991) 'Political connections, professional advancement, and moral education in Durkheimian sociology', *Journal of the History of the Behavioral Sciences* 27:56–75.

Chapter 7

Suicide and anomie

Philippe Besnard

'Suicide' and 'anomie' – here we have two stimuli which immediately conjure up the Durkheimian heritage for any sociologist or student of sociology. The combination of the two stimuli, 'Suicide' and 'anomie', seems very banal today, simply because the Durkheimian theory of anomie has been particularly developed in *Le Suicide* (1897a). Many scholarly interpretations of this book have a mistaken tendency to see anomie as 'the cause of suicide' by confusing egoistic suicide with anomic suicide, or actually by making anomie a generic idea embracing diverse social pathologies. It has not always been so. For a long time interpretations, discussions or utilizations of Durkheim's book neglected anomie, either by ignoring this aspect of Durkheimian theory completely or by rejecting it in a few lines. A book by the Durkheimian Halbwachs, *Les Causes du Suicide* (1930), is the most perfect example of this silence mixed with rejection.

The American sociology of the 1930s, particularly in Chicago, so preoccupied with 'social problems', 'social disorganization', 'social pathology', totally ignored the notion of anomie and more generally the Durkheimian theory of suicide.

'Suicide and anomie' is the title of a chapter in a book published in 1962, intended to present the classics of empirical sociology (Madge 1962). Twenty-four years earlier, the monumental history of social thought by Becker and Barnes (1938) contained only one furtive allusion to normlessness in the summary they gave of *Le Suicide*. In the interim there was the impact of Parsons's book, *The Structure of Social Action* (1937);

and the impact, too, of the famous work by Merton on the theme of 'social structure and anomie'. Above all, the English translation of *Le Suicide* appeared in 1951 which was crucial for disseminating the word *anomie* as well as for the new interest in the sociology of suicide. The best example of this is the book by Henry and Short (1954), which explicitly sets out to test the Durkheimian hypothesis of economic anomie. At the end of the 1950s conceptual studies on the Durkheimian theory of suicide proliferated in parallel with empirical works on the subject. In the 1960s *Le Suicide* acquired the status of a 'classic' and anomie was then considered as the sociological concept *par excellence*, that is, both as a notion central to the discipline and as a word to which sociologists had a prior claim. The problem is that the same word had varied and even contradictory meanings (Besnard 1987).

'Suicide and anomie' – let me justify this title yet again by noting that the empirical works on suicide, like studies making use of the concept (or the word) 'anomie', have in common ritual and obligatory references to Durkheim. These are two areas where the Durkheimian heritage appears direct and not diffuse.

'Suicide and anomie' – this title is in fact a little misleading, because for the past thirty years the sociological literature on suicide has forgotten anomie even more than before. In a recent set of essays on *Le Suicide*, very little reference is made to anomie (Pickering and Walford 2000). This trend is confirmed by the selected article by K. D. Breault who draws up a balance sheet of recent studies of suicide [Breault]. Interest is becoming increasingly focused on egoistic suicide and more specifically on the question of the relationship between religion and suicide. Breault himself was one of the principal representatives of the trend in research which makes use of ecological correlations. In the text reprinted here, however, he proclaims his renunciation of this type of approach, stating that there is no justification for an ecological study of suicide and adopting the formula 'no more aggregate studies' as one of the 'new rules of sociological method'. The article by Besnard, 'Marriage and suicide' belongs to a less well-explored genre since it attempts to test the present validity of the Durkheimian theory of conjugal anomie applied to recent data on suicide in France [P. Besnard 2000].

Le Suicide also contains a theory of the two dimensions of the theory of the social bond, i.e. integration and regulation (and see Chapter 8). The question of the difference between these two dimensions has long been the subject of debate among the interpreters of Durkheim. Those who support the idea were in the majority in the 1960s and 1970s. The most recent interpretations of Durkheim, on the contrary, admit the autonomy of these two dimensions of the social bond (notably, Besnard 1987, Cherkaoui 1998, Steiner 1998). This debate arises because Durkheim did not formulate the theory of regulation (anomie-fatalism) in as coherent and complete a way as the theory of integration. Besnard's text, 'Anomie and fatalism' suggests a reconstruction of this latter theory [Besnard 1993].

The most innovative recent developments in Durkheimian scholarship on suicide are, it seems, the study of the sources of the book and its intellectual context. A few samples of this will be found here. First of all the relationship with statistics, because Durkheim's book rests on a tradition of moral statistics that had developed throughout the nineteenth century and which had taken suicide as a favourite subject of study. Turner's article shows in a new way what Durkheim's methodology and his conception of causality owe to the statisticians of the time, but also how they differ from them [Turner].

Le Suicide is to a considerable extent a book directed against the man whom Durkheim regarded as his principal adversary, Gabriel Tarde (Besnard 1995). Starting out from Durkheim's letters to Tarde, Massimo Borlandi undertakes a meticulous investigation into the state of the conflict between the two men up to the moment when Durkheim wrote *Le Suicide* and also contributes new views on the stages in the writing of the book, an important matter in understanding the work [Borlandi].

An aspect which has been completely neglected until recent years is Durkheim's relationship to the 'alienist' literature on suicide (see also Mucchielli and Renneville 1998). According to Berrios and Mohanna, Durkheim gave a presentation of the psychiatric conception of suicide in the nineteenth century which is not only a caricature but false as well [Berrios and Mohanna]. An article by Joséphine Besnard, focusing on Brierre de Boismont, Durkheim's principal psychiatric source, qualifies this vision and seeks to explain why Durkheim chose to confront the extreme alienist theory (the theory which views all suicide as an act of mental alienation) rather than the moderate alienist thesis, which was much more dangerous since it competed with the sociological discipline that Durkheim wanted to establish [J. Besnard].

Alasdair MacIntyre, the well-known philosopher who has a considerable interest in sociology, wrote in 1978 a critical article on *Le Suicide*. He underlined Durkheim's failure to take into account the intentions of the person committing suicide and also that Durkheim was a 'positivist'. As with so many of the criticisms that have arisen since the publication of the book, issues about method have been prominent. Strikwerda challenges MacIntyre on a number of points, for example, that Durkheim was not a positivist in the Comtean sense, nor a Humean in the matter of causation [Strikwerda]. Rather than trying to find universal laws, Durkheim attempted to discover 'general schema'. Further, Durkheim was not opposed to the idea of intentionality but found it inadequate for his purposes. Finally, Strikwerda relates the ideas of Durkheim and MacIntrye to the suicide of Socrates.

Finally, as W. S. F. Pickering recalls, Durkheim's *Le Suicide* is not just about trying to explain suicide sociologically [Pickering]. Larger issues emerge throughout the book but most notably in the final chapters. One issue in question is that Durkheim leaps over the boundary line of the 'scientific' and becomes a dogmatic moralist. Following what some see as a Christian and Catholic point of view, Durkheim, as an agnostic and a rationalist, upholds the position that suicide, except altruistic suicide, is an immoral act and one to be condemned. His condemnation is in part due to the fact that he sees with alarm what he considers to be high levels of suicide in Western Europe as a manifestation of *le malaise social*. Further, he tries to show that suicide is immoral in the light of what he foresees as the future secular religion, namely, the cult of the individual.

References

Becker, H. and Barnes, H. E. (1938) *Social Thought from Lore to Science*, New York: Heath.

Besnard, P. (1987) *L'Anomie, ses usages et ses fonctions dans la discipline sociologique depuis Durkheim*, Paris: Presses Universitaires de France.

Besnard, P. (1995) 'Durkheim critique de Tarde; des *Règles* au *Suicide*', in M. Borlandi et L. Mucchielli (eds) *La sociologie et sa méthode. Les Règles de Durkheim un siècle après*, Paris: L'Harmattan.

Cherkaoui, M. (1998) *Naissance d'une science sociale. La sociologie selon Durkheim*, Genève: Droz.

Durkheim, E. (1897a) *Le Suicide: étude de sociologie*, Paris: Alcan.

— (t.1951a) by J. A. Spaulding and G. Simpson, *Suicide: a study in sociology*, Glencoe, Ill.: Free Press of Glencoe.

Halbwachs, M. (1930) *Les Causes du suicide*, Paris: Alcan.

Henry, A. F. and Short, J. F. (1954) *Suicide and Homicide*, Glencoe, Ill.: Free Press.

Madge, J. (1962) *The Origins of Scientific Sociology*, New York: Free Press of Glencoe.

Mucchielli, L. et Renneville, M. (1998) 'Les causes du suicide: pathologie individuelle ou sociale? Halbwachs et les psychiatres de leur temps (1830–1930)', *Déviance et société* 22(1):3–36.

Parsons, T. (1937) *The Structure of Social Action*, New York: Free Press.

Pickering, W. S. F. and Walford, G. (eds) (2000) *Durkheim's Suicide: a century of research and debate*, London: Routledge.

Steiner, P. (1998) *La sociologie de Durkheim*, Paris: La Découverte.

Selected Items

Berrios, G. E. and Mohanna, M. (1990) 'Durkheim and French psychiatric views on suicide during the 19th century: a conceptual history', *British Journal of Psychiatry* 156:1–9.

Besnard, J. (2000) 'La référence aliéniste de Durkheim: Alexandre Brierre de Boisment', in M. Borlandi and M. Cherkaoui (eds), *Le suicide de Durkheim une siècle après*, Paris: Presses Universitaires de France.

Besnard, P. (1993) 'Anomie and fatalism in Durkheim's theory of regulation', in S. Turner (ed.), *Emile Durkheim. Sociologist and Moralist*, London: Routledge.

Besnard, P. (2000) 'Marriage and suicide: testing the Durkheimian theory of marital regulation a century later', in W. S. F. Pickering and G. Walford (eds), *Durkheim's Suicide: a century of research and debate*, London: Routledge.

Borlandi, M. (1994) 'Informations sur la rédaction du *Suicide* et sur l'état du conflit entre Durkheim et Tarde de 1895 à 1897', *Etudes durkheimiennes/Durkheim Studies* VI:4–13.

Breault, K. D. (1994) 'Was Durkheim right? A critical survey of the empirical literature on *Le Suicide*', in D. Lester (ed.), *Emile Durkheim. Le Suicide. One Hundred Years Later, International Sociology*, pp. 11–29.

Pickering, W. S. F. (2000) 'Reading the Conclusion: *Suicide*, morality and religion', in W. S. F. Pickering and G. Walford (eds), *Durkheim's Suicide: a century of research and debate*, London: Routledge.

Strikwerda, R. A. (1997) 'An analysis of Alisdair MacIntyre's 'Notes on Durkheim's *Suicide*', *Durkheimian Studies/Etudes Durkheimiennes*, n.s., 3:59–72.

Turner, S. (1996) 'Durkheim among the statisticians', *Journal of the History of the Behavioral Sciences* 32(4):354–78.

Chapter 8

Division of labour and economics

Philippe Steiner

De la Division du travail social was Durkheim's main doctoral thesis and first book and is seminal (1893b). This is particularly true when the connections between political economy and sociology are the focus of enquiry. Two dimensions will be considered in this chapter. First, we shall give a brief overview of Durkheim's position on political economy and his legacy to economic sociology. Second, as the division of labour is closely connected to exchange and contract, political economy and law we shall point to two facets of any such sociological enquiry. It is still worth considering the strength and weaknesses of Durkheim's sociological approach to law and economics at a moment when economic sociology is becoming a strategic research area (Steiner 1999a) and economists are ready to take into account many moral and social facts that were ruled out some decades ago.[1]

Political economy and the sociological approach

In the first period of his academic career, which was between 1885 and 1896 and which was focused on his doctorate, Durkheim was busy acquainting himself with the literature on political economy.[2] After Adam Smith's famous chapters on the division of labour, there had been a steady flow of research on the topic. Charles Babbage's study of 1832 on machines and manufacture was a major step in this area; Karl Marx in 1867 provided another one with his distinction between manufacture and industry in terms of labour processes; Frederic W. Taylor's

studies on work and plant organization offered a third development at the end of the nineteenth century. However, Durkheim
was not much interested in what really happened within the
factory or between industries – the only proviso to be made in
this respect is related to the last part of the *Division du travail
social* in which he commented briefly on three (in fact four)
unsatisfactory situations in the working process. Instead, he
focused on the moral and sociological side of the subject – a
topic still on the political economists agenda, particularly
within the German Historical School.[3] This last current of
thought seemed more relevant to Durkheim, who was fully
aware of it owing to his stay in Germany during the academic
year 1885–86 (Lukes 1973, chap. 4; Steiner 1994). Durkheim's
interests in political economy remained important until the end
of the nineteenth century as is shown by the numerous references he made to this social science in his lectures on socialism
(Durkheim 1928a). However, he was then closer to 'heterodox'
political economy, like the one provided by Jean Charles
Léonard Simonde de Sismondi and, more than anyone else, by
Henri Saint-Simon and the Saint-Simonians. The reason is
plain: they provided him with an economic analysis which did
not leave out the concerns raised by the relation between the
material and the moral organization of modern society.

After this period, political economy was no longer of interest
to Durkheim who almost completely left out the domain from
the range of his enquiries. This is probably due to its failure to
produce a method for a study of political economy,[4] and also to
his new and keen interest in the sociology of religion and
anthropology.

This brief account of Durkheim's relations with political
economy reveals that he was at variance with two great thinkers
of the time whose names are strongly connected with classical
sociology. Vilfredo Pareto and Max Weber were economists (as a
matter of fact, Pareto was an engineer and Weber was a lawyer)
and, to say the least, Durkheim's knowledge was certainly weak
compared with theirs (Gislain and Steiner 1995), even if there

exist some interesting similarities with the American institutionalists (Gislain and Steiner 1999), particularly on the methodological critique of political economy.

Durkheim wrongly believed that the mainstream political economy of his time was not concerned with morals, but only with the material side of the division of labour. He paid the price of his misperception of political economy, since he could have found many 'orthodox' economists who lamented the social inequalities existing in the market and who provided possible solutions (unions, associations, and the like) to this most serious problem.[5] As Besnard rightly points out, this limitation of Durkheim's knowledge is apparent in the last part of the *Division du travail social* (Besnard *et al.* 1993). There, Durkheim was less accurate in his judgements and, more important, he did not analyse carefully the situation of the workers in the factory. Consequently, he missed the fact that the so-called abnormal forms of the division of labour (inequalities, anomie, bureaucracy, over-separation in the work process, to use Besnard's terminology), appear to us as normal forms.

Therefore, one may wonder about Durkheim's impact on political economy and economic sociology. Surprisingly enough, this impact was indirect but strong. François Simiand (1873–1935) and Maurice Halbwachs (1877–1944), two outstanding scholars belonging to the Durkheimian school (Besnard 1983), fulfilled the promises of Durkheimian ideas as the fifth section of the *L'Année sociologique* illustrates.[6] After the First World War, the two Durkheimians became famous economic sociologists thanks to their studies on wages (Simiand 1907; 1932), on money (Simiand 1934), on consumption (Halbwachs 1913; 1933) and on social classes (Halbwachs 1940).[7] After the Second World War, their influence was weaker and the economists (for example, André Marchal 1951–5) were then reluctant to pay their debt to Durkheim and the Durkheimians.[8] But their leading ideas are still influential within two contemporary currents of French political economy,[9] which stress the role of the institutional and historical settings of economics.

The emphasis put on the social embeddedness of economic behaviour was a crucial concern of the Durkheimians. As a matter of fact, they were persuaded that it was not possible to understand individual economic action outside the economic context – its institutional aspects (either formal institutions as contractual law, regulation of work and wages, or mental institutions, that is representations, as feelings of justice (Durkheim) or trust (Simiand; Halbwachs)). Even there connections exist between the Durkheimian approach and new institutionalism (Williamson 1985). The differences are more important since the Durkheimians strongly rejected the maximization principle as an explanation of the rational selection of economic institutions. This raises the problem of the nature of economic and societal changes and the place given to evolutionary theories in Durkheim's thought.

This aspect of the Durkheimian research programme has been studied by C. Limoges and M. Hawkins [Limoges; Hawkins]. They show that within Durkheim's works there exist strong analogies between biological sciences and sociology, precisely when the problems raised by social change are at stake. This connection was not uncommon in that period dominated by Herbert Spencer's sociological works, but Limoges reminds the reader that the Darwinian principle of selection was itself grounded on a social science analogy, that is, the Malthusian theory of population growth. However, according to Limoges, Durkheim's achievements do not stand high in this domain. Hawkins considers in depth a part of this general problem and shows convincingly that while using biological analogies, Durkheim was not guilty of a reductionist strategy according to which sociological explanation of evolution would be similar to a biological one. Sociological processes are specific and ask for a true sociological explanation as Durkheim strongly stated in the first and fifth chapters of his *Règles de la méthode sociologique* (1895a). In this respect, Durkheim's lecture on contract and property rights (Durkheim 1950a) or on the institutional evolution of education (Durkheim 1938a) are still worth considering.

Political economy, law and sociology

As is apparent in the *Division du travail social,* three social sciences are closely knit together: sociology, law and economics. If we set aside the institutional connections between them in France in that period,[10] we may first focus on Durkheim's sociological approach to law, an approach that was different, but less systematic than the one developed later on by Max Weber, whose emphasis was on the various historical rationalization processes at work in Europe (Weber 1921). Chazel's paper makes clear that the Durkheimian programme of sociology of law was not fully developed in his first book and some important changes were introduced later on [Chazel]. Particularly he points to an essay published in *L'Année sociologique* ('Les deux Lois de l'évolution pénale') in 1901 and through the steady work on the third section of his review devoted to moral and juridical sociology. Durkheim's sociology of law had three objects: first, the juridical practices actually carried out; second, the juridical institutions in such and such domain of modern life and, finally, the whole institutional setting provided by all these juridical institutions. Chazel is right when he explains that this sociology of law was missing something important, namely the problem raised by the construction of juridical institutions. However, Durkheim's famous analysis of crime as being 'normal' is of interest in this respect as Garland argues [Garland]. Punishment then appears as a mechanism producing social solidarity through the penalty placed upon the offender but also through the satisfaction given to the part of the collective consciousness which had been injured.

Beyond these concerns related to the scope of Durkheim's sociology of law, political economy, law and sociology are strongly connected at a theoretical level. Is the normative side of human behaviour of any value when studying economic problems? Are there any reasons to make a great divide between rules, conventions and norms and the teleological behaviour of the self-interested economic agent?

Durkheim's answer to the first question is positive. Yes, the normative side of economic behaviour is important since modern social cohesion cannot be provided by self-interested action alone. In Chapter 7 of the *Division du travail social*, Durkheim wrote a strong critique of Spencer's ideas when he used an argument similar to the one employed by Adam Smith in order to explain the benefits resulting from the impersonal mechanism of market exchanges. Durkheim went further, since he believed that social representations are important if one wants to understand the actual economic behaviour of people. For example, social representations of justice are, according to Durkheim, of the utmost importance in order to understand the growth of the contract considered as an institutional corner-stone of modernity (Durkheim 1950a:231). The same is true when Durkheim explained in his *Division du travail social* and in his *Suicide* (1897a) that a social evaluation (*évaluation sociale*) of the revenues distributed was at the root of the feeling of justice among the bulk of the people. In other words, there exist inequalities that are socially considered as normal (in Durkheim's meaning of that word) and others that are offensive to the social conscience because a too large (or too small) revenue is the reward received by a class of people for the social function they perform. This element is captured, respectively, by Beckert and Steiner in their articles, which deal with Durkheim's point of view on political economy [Beckert; Steiner]. Beckert is right when he explains that Durkheim's theory is not completely convincing since there is no real explanation of the price mechanism in terms of normative behaviour offered by the French sociologist. However, following Beckert's conclusions does not mean that Durkheim's ideas should be left out in contemporary economic sociology. His ideas on economic justice are of interest for a theory of collective action since they may explain why in some specific circumstances people react or do not react when confronted by massive economic inequalities.[11] Furthermore, contemporary economists are now more inclined to consider the normative side of economic behaviour. This is particularly true when the labour market is concerned. The high levels of unemployment over a long period of time is a salient fact that prevents economists from sticking to textbook explanations of the clearing mechanism, consequently some of them introduce sociological and normative elements in the behavioural hypotheses of their models. According to the Nobel prize winner Robert Solow (1990), economists cannot make a model of the labour market without taking into account the social representations of justice that are in the minds of the workers. Thus, Solow suggests an economic explanation in which it is socially rational for workers not to undersell their colleagues (and thus to prevent the market from providing a clearing up of demand and supply) and to stick to the normal effort/wages ratio.

The second question raises a major problem in contemporary social science. Are norms the result of self-interested behaviour? If a positive answer is given to the question, then the Durkheimian approach would be severely undermined, since normative behaviour and the corresponding institutions could and would be reduced to individual actions and strategies. To the best of our knowledge, it seems that there does not exist any definitive answer to such a question[12] and, most often, social scientists consider that some rules and norms may be rationally explained by explicit self-interested behaviour. However, in other instances, even with the conjectural analysis provided by evolutionary games theory, this is not possible. In which case, rules and norms cannot be explained as resulting from an agreement between self-interested actors. If we consider specifically economic norms, it is worth emphasizing the results provided by T. C. Schelling's analysis of pure co-ordination problems (e.g. the choice between the left or right lane for drivers) (Schelling 1977). There exist problems (formalized in terms of games theory) in which two (at least) equilibria are available and rational behaviour cannot provide the solution, which depends on the contrary anticipations made by the people involved. In that case, Schelling suggests that a solution will be grounded on the stock of common values, salient beliefs and the like.

This last example inevitably takes us back to the Durkheimian approach. However, the approach should be modified in one important respect owing to the curious blindness of Durkheim and his school. It is well known that these scholars relentlessly rejected what they called the finalist interpretation of social behaviour. To put it in a nut shell, they reacted negatively to any explanation of social facts grounded in rational actors behaving in a particular way to achieve their goals. According to their positivistic conception of science, this explanation is vitiated by a teleological fallacy,[13] since social phenomena would then be considered as logical outcomes of intentional action. There is no reason to follow them down this cul-de-sac. Norms, rules and institutions are most of the time *unanticipated outcomes of intentional actions*. In other words, the Durkheimian approach should be enlarged to make room for processes of rule and norm formation in which actors' strategies are *one* element of sociological explanation. In this respect, the paper by Reynaud is a highly innovative piece of work [Reynaud]. He stresses the fact that a theory of rule formation is available in Durkheim's *Division du travail social* when one considers that solidarity can be seen not as a result of a social need, but as a social construction in which actors (whether individuals or not) build the rules. These rules are not necessarily the best solutions, that is the most useful or most efficient, they are devices that allow the set of actors to maintain their social cohesion. Reynaud adds, and this is important, that when a rule is found then it is indeed compelling to follow the rule, but as the rule cannot give an answer to any problems that may happen in the future, the rule may be modified through implicit or explicit negotiations between actors. Rules and norms thus become processes out of which solidarity results.

Division of labour, economic sociology and reform

If Durkheim's concerns were not strongly oriented towards phenomena occurring within the factory or within the market, they were towards social reform; this is the main theme of an article by W. Watts-Miller [Watts Miller]. Durkheim made a bold claim when he stated in the second preface of the *Division du travail social* that his researches would not be worth the time they cost him if they could not provide any practical orientations or reforms. In what way did Durkheim offer anything positive?

In the first preface of his major doctoral thesis (1893b), Durkheim stressed that a science of morals could be useful in making it easier to fit social values into modern society. In line with the concluding remarks of *Le suicide* (1897a), the second preface for the 1902 edition of his thesis suggested that French and European social problems lay in the weakness of social integration, particularly within the economic domain. Corporations could provide a solution through integrative (social interaction between workers and management, etc.) and regulative mechanisms (definition of wages hierarchy, etc.) by producing a stronger social cohesion. Watts-Miller shows convincingly that Durkheim's point of view was innovative, even if he failed in this respect.[14]

As the material basis of the division of labour has changed at a rapid pace, one may ask with Neil J. Smelser: is it not that the nation-state is losing its grip in favour of large-scale political construction on the one hand, and on the small-scale community on the other [Smelser]? For many European peoples now, it is plain that there exists a new and larger political construction (the European Community) that modifies in depth the role of each national state in terms of socialization, economic socialization included.[15] It is also plain that below the level of national State, there still exist forms of social life (organized around language, ethnicity, regional tradition, and the like)[16] that remain important or, even become more and more important for the socialization of contemporary men and women in Europe. In this respect, as Smelser suggests, the Durkheimian approach is probably still of interest for studying the relationships between social differentiation and social cohesion, even if the present forms are no longer the same as the one that Durkheim studied more than one century ago.

Notes

1. See, for example, the paper delivered by the Nobel prize winner, Amartya Sen (1998), in which mortality is considered as an indicator of economic performance. Any reader of the *Division du travail social* who has in mind Durkheim's definition of suicide as an indicator of well-being (Durkheim 1893b; 1897a), will be struck by the similarities (and differences as well) between this approach of a major social problem (famines and food shortages) and Durkheim's approach to socio-economic problems of his time.

2. Some evidence is available in a paper devoted to the books that the young Durkheim read in the Ecole Normale Supérieure (Paoletti 1992). Other evidences are provided by Logue (1994) and Steiner (1994).

3. This is particularly the case with Karl Bücher, Gustav Schmoller and Adolf Wagner – see also the references provided by Maurice Block (1897) in the opening chapter of his book devoted to giving a general overview of the achievements of political economists since Adam Smith. The German Historical School was important for the Durkheimians in the beginning of the twentieth century where economic sociology is concerned (see Bouglé 1907, Chapter 4; Bouglé and Raffault 1930), even if Simiand and Halbwachs were critical of this school (Steiner 1998b).

4. The deductive method is criticized in the second chapter of the *Règles de la méthode sociologique* (1895a). According to Durkheim, the so-called law of demand and supply was not a result of experimental approach, but a logical result of deductive analysis. Later on (May 1896), he wrote to Bouglé that the study of political economy left him a negative feeling. However, he added that with the help

of statistics and history, there were certainly major discoveries to be made in that domain (Durkheim 1975b, II: 392).

5. See for example Jean-Baptiste Say (1803) and Charles Dupond-White (1846) in France and see William Thornton (1869) on wages formation and John Stuart Mill's recantation after his reading of this book (Mill 1869).

6. This section was important in the first series of *L'Année sociologique* (1898–1913); it was still important in the second series (1924–26) and constituted a substantial part (série D) of the set of series published under the slightly modified title *Annales sociologiques* (1932–40).

7. In this respect, various recent studies on French economic sociology or *économie positive* are available (Gillard and Rosier 1996, Gislain and Steiner 1999, Steiner 1998a, 1999b, Frobert 2000).

8. However, a doctoral thesis written under the supervision of A. Marchal, which was to evaluate the interest of Durkheim's ideas for political economy, was then published (Aimard 1962).

9. For the school known as '*Ecole de la régulation*', see Boyer (1986) or Boyer and Saillard (1995) for general assessments on the school; and Steiner (forthcoming) for a historical study of Boyer's research programme and its connections with Durkheimian economic sociology. For the school known as '*Economie des conventions*', see the special issue by the *Revue Economique* 2, 1989.

10. The reader should keep in mind that during Durkheim's lifetime, political economy and law were taught within the Faculté de Droit, whereas the little teaching of sociology in French universities was located in the Faculté de Lettres. Institutionalization of sociology was on Durkheim's agenda and that was not an easy task to fulfil. We now know he was not really successful in this respect (Karady 1976, 1979).

11. One may associate this sociological approach by Durkheim and the *sociological* side of the historical work carried out by Edward P. Thompson about crowds in time of food shortages (Thompson 1971).

12. See, for example, at the symposium organized by the *Journal of Economic Perspectives*, Richard Sugden (1989) explained the results of the approach of games theory and Jon Elster (1989) expresses doubts concerning the possibility of extending such an explanation to *all* social norms.

13. I would add two caveats to this statement. First, Halbwachs is probably less guilty in this respect (see, for example, his arguments against the neglect of motives by Durkheim (Halbwachs 1930, Introduction)). It is not by chance that he was so much interested in the sociological approach offered by Weber (Steiner 1999b). Second, following Raymond Boudon's analysis of Durkheim's last book (Boudon 1999), or Mohamed Cherkaoui's general interpretation (Cherkaoui 1998), Durkheim himself was not always reluctant to take into account the motives of the actor. The same remark applies to Simiand's work on wages (Steiner 1996).

14. After Durkheim's death, corporations were left out by Durkheimian economic sociologists. Simiand's analysis of the American industrial situation, made it clear that unions were a necessary element of modern economic systems since workers had to negotiate conditions of labour and wages with trusts and large companies. He added that these unions were new institutions that had nothing to do with corporations, since workers and bosses did not belong to the same union (Simiand 1928–31, 2, lectures 31–2).

15. See, for example, the paper by Fligstein and Mara-Drita (1997) on the social construction of the European market and the complex relationships between this supra-national level and the national States about the legal economic system to be built for making homogeneous the European market.

16. Taking ethnicity as an example, one can find in Alejandro Portes's book many connections between the macro-level (immigration) and micro-level (ethnic networks and entrepreneurship) when jobs are concerned (Portes 1995). The micro-level is also present in the conclusion of Mark Granovetter's famous study (Granovetter 1995).

References

Aimard, G. (1962) *Durkheim et la science économique*, Paris: Presses Universitaires de France.

Besnard, P. (ed.) (1983) *The Sociological Domain: the Durkheimians and the Founding of French sociology*, Cambridge: Cambridge University Press.

Besnard, P., Borlandi, M. and Vogt, P. (eds) (1993) *Division du travail et lien social. Durkheim un siècle après*, Paris: Presses Universitaires de France.

Block, M. (1897) *Les Progrès de la science économique depuis Adam Smith*, Paris: Guillaumin.

Boudon, R. (1999) 'Les Formes élémentaires de la vie religieuse: une théorie toujours vivante', *L'Année sociologique* 1:149–98.

Bouglé, C. (1907) *Qu'est-ce que la sociologie*, Paris: Alcan.

Bouglé, C. and Raffault, J. (1930) *Eléments de sociologie. Textes choisis et ordonnés*, Paris: Alcan.

Boyer, R. (1986) *La Théorie de la régulation: une analyse critique*, Paris: La Découverte.

Boyer, R. and Saillard, Y. (eds) (1995) *La Théorie de la régulation. L'état des savoirs*, Paris: La Découverte.

Cherkaoui, M. (1998) *Naissance d'une science sociale. La sociologie selon Durkheim*, Genève: Droz.

Dupond-White, C. (1846) *Essai sur les relations du travail avec le capital*, Paris: Guillaumin.

Durkheim, E. (1893b) *De la Division du travail social*, Paris: Presses Universitaires de France (1973 ed.).

— (1895a) *Les Règles de la méthode sociologique*, Paris: Alcan.

— (1897a) *Le Suicide*, Paris: Alcan.

— (1928a) *Le Socialisme*, Paris: Alcan.

— (1938a) *L'Evolution pédagogique en France*, 2 vols, Paris: Presses Universitaires de France.

— (1950a) *Leçons de sociologie*, Paris: Presses Universitaires de France.

— (1975b) *Emile Durkheim: Textes*, 3 vols, V. Karady (ed.) Paris: Minuit.

Elster, J. (1989) 'Social norms and economic theory', *Journal of Economic Perspectives* 3:99–117.

Fligstein, N. and Mara-Drita, I. (1997) 'How to make a market: reflections on the European Community's Single Market Program', *American Journal of Sociology* 1:1–33.

Frobert, L. (2000) *Le Travail de François Simiand (1873–1935)*, Paris: Economica.

Gillard, L. and Rosier, M. (eds) (1996) *François Simiand (1873–1935). Sociologie-Histoire-Economie*, Amsterdam: Editions des Archives contemporaines.

Gislain, J.-J. and Steiner, P. (1995) *La Sociologie économique (1890–1920): E. Durkheim, V. Pareto, J. Schumpeter, F. Simiand, T. Veblen et M. Weber*, Paris: Presses Universitaires de France.

Gislain, J.-J. and Steiner, P. (1999) 'American institutionalism and Durkheimian positive economics: some connections', *History of Political Economy* 31: 273–96.

Granovetter, M. (1995) *Getting a Job*, 2nd edn, Chicago: Chicago University Press.

Halbwachs, M. (1913) *La Classe ouvrière et les niveaux de vie*, London: Gordon & Breach.

Halbwachs, M. (1930) *Les Causes du suicide*, Paris: Alcan.

Halbwachs, M. (1933) *L'Evolution des besoins dans les classes ouvrières*, Paris: Alcan.

Halbwachs, M. (1940) *Sociologie économique et démographie*, Paris: Hermann.

Karady, V. (1976) 'Durkheim, les sciences sociales et l'Université: bilan d'un semi échec', *Revue française de sociologie* 2:267–312.

Karady, V. (1979) 'Stratégies de réussite et modes de faire valoir de la sociologie chez les durkheimiens', *Revue française de sociologie* 1:49–82.

Logue, W. (1994) 'Durkheim et les économistes français', in P. Besnard, M. Borlandi and P. Vogt (eds) *Division du travail et lien social. Durkheim un siècle après*, Paris: Presses Universitaires.

Lukes, S. (1973) *Emile Durkheim. His Life and Work. A Historical and Critical Study*, London: The Penguin Press.

Marchal, A. (1951–5) *Méthode scientifique et science économique*, Paris: Médicis.

Mill, J. S. (1869) 'Thornton on Labour and its Claims', *The Collected Works of John Stuart Mill*, vol.5, London: Routledge.

Paoletti, G. (1992) 'Durkheim à l'Ecole Normale Supérieure: lectures de jeunesse', *Etudes durkheimiennes/Durkheim Studies* 4:9–21.

Portes, A. (ed.) (1995) *The Sociology of Immigration. Essays on networks, ethnicity and entrepreneurship*, New York: Russel Sage Foundation.

Reynaud, J.-D. (1989) *Les Règles du jeu. L'action collective et la régulation sociale*, Paris: A. Colin.

Say, J.-B. (1803) *Traité d'économie politique*, Paris: Crapelet.

Schelling, T. C. (1977) *The Strategy of Conflict*, Oxford: Oxford University Press.

Sen, A. (1998) 'Mortality as an indicator of economic success or failure', *The Economic Journal* 108:1–25.

Simiand, F. (1907) *Le Salaire dans l'industrie des mines en France et au XIXe siècle*, Paris: Cornély.

Simiand, F. (1928–1931) *Cours d'économie politique*, Paris: Domat-Montchrestien.

Simiand, F. (1932) *Le Salaire, l'évolution sociale et la monnaie*, Paris: Alcan.

Simiand, F. (1934) 'La monnaie, réalité sociale', *Annales sociologiques*, série D, 1:1–81.

Solow, R. (1990) *The Labor Market as a Social Institution*, Oxford: Blackwell.

Steiner, P. (1994) 'Durkheim, les économistes et la critique de l'économie politique', *Economia* 19:135–59.

Steiner, P. (1996) 'Notes sur la théorie de l'action sous-jacente au dilemme production/répartition', in L. Gillard and M. Rosier (eds) *François Simiand (1873–1935). Sociologie – Histoire – Economie*, Amsterdam: Editions des Archives contemporaines: 195–200.

Steiner, P. (1998a) 'La sociologie économique comme critique de l'économie politique', *L'Année sociologique* 48:115–37.

Steiner, P. (1998b) 'Durkheim's Sociology, Simiand's Positive Political Economy and the German Historical School', King's College, Cambridge, discussion paper (forthcoming).

Steiner, P. (1999a) *La Sociologie économique*, Paris: La Découverte.

Steiner, P. (1999b) 'Maurice Halbwachs: les derniers feux de la sociologie économique durkheimienne', *Revue d'histoire des sciences humaines* 1:141–62.

Steiner, P. (forthcoming) 'L'économie américaine et le fordisme. De Simiand à l'Ecole de la régulation', *L'Année de la régulation*.

Sugden, R. (1989) 'Spontaneous Order', *Journal of Economic Perspectives* 3:85–97.

Thompson, E. P. (1971) 'The Moral Economy of the English Crowd in the Eighteenth Century', *Past and Present* 4:76–136.

Thornton, W. (1869) *On Labour. Its Wrongful Claims and Rightful Dues. Its Actual Present and Possible Future*, London: Macmillan.

Wallwork, E. (1975) *Durkheim. Morality and Milieu*, Cambridge Mass.: Harvard University Press.

Weber, M. (1921) *Economy and Society*. English translation, Berkeley: The University of California Press (1978).

Williamson, O. E. (1985) *The Institutions of Capitalism*, New York: The Free Press.

Selected Items

Beckert, J. (1997) 'Contract and social justice: Emile Durkheim's theory of integration of modern societies', *Kolner Zeitschrift für Sociologie, und Sozialpsychologie* 49(4):629–49.

Besnard, P. (1993) 'Les pathologies des sociétés modernes', in M. Borlandi, P. Besnard and W. Vogt (eds), *Division du travail et lien social*, Paris: Presses Universitaires de France.

Chazel, F. (1991) 'Emile Durkheim et l'élaboration d'un "programme de recherche" en sociologie du droit', in F. Chazel and J. Commaille (eds), *Normes juridiques et régulation sociale*, Paris: Montchrestien.

Garland, D. (1999) 'Durkheim's sociology of punishment and punishment today', in M. S. Cladis (ed.), *Durkheim and Foucault: perspectives on education and punishment*, Oxford: Durkheim Press.

Hawkins, M. (1999) 'Durkheim's sociology and theories of degeneration', *Economy and Society* 28(1):118–37.

Limoges, C. (1994) 'Milne-Edwards, Darwin, Durkheim and *The Division of Labour*: a case study in reciprocal conceptual exchanges between the social and natural sciences', in I. B. Cohen (ed.), *The Natural Sciences and the Social Sciences*, Dordrecht and London: Kluwer Academic.

Reynaud, J.-D. (1993) 'La formation des règles sociales', in M. Borlandi, P. Besnard and W. Vogt (eds), *Division du travail et lien social*, Paris: Presses Universitaires de France.

Smelser, N. J. (1993) 'The problematic link between differentiation and integration', in M. Borlandi, P. Besnard and W. Vogt (eds), *Division du travail et lien social*, Paris: Presses Universitaires de France.

Steiner, P. (1992) 'Le fait social économique chez Durkheim', *Revue française de sociologie* XXXIII:641–61.

Watts Miller, W. (1993) 'Les deux préfaces: science morale et réforme sociale', in M. Borlandi, P. Besnard and W. Vogt (eds), *Division du travail et lien social*, Paris: Presses Universitaires de France.

Chapter 9

Education

Geoffrey Walford

In 1977 Jerome Karabel and A. H. Halsey published their highly authoritative edited collection of articles, *Power and Ideology of Education*. This text was designed to delineate for the late 1970s and 1980s the scope and achievements of sociology of education in Britain and the United States in a similar way as Halsey, Floud and Anderson's (1961) previous collection *Education, Economy and Society* had done for the 1960s. It did so with great success and the book became an essential text for any student taking sociology of education courses in either country.

Following a long introductory review which summarized and interpreted the condition and future of sociology of education at that time, Karabel and Halsey chose, for their first substantive chapter called 'On Education and Society', a translation of part of Durkheim's *The Evolution of Educational Thought*, which was extracted from the then forthcoming translation by Peter Collins (Durkheim 1938a/t.1977a). That they should put Durkheim at the forefront of this volume of contemporary research and scholarship on education is remarkable, and it signals at least a temporary resurgence of interest in Durkheim's educational work. Even more remarkable is the fact that within their long introduction they suggest that Durkheim's theoretical framework, as it had been interpreted and developed by Basil Bernstein, offered 'a new synthesis' between normative and interpretive approaches to sociology of education, and between macro- and micro-considerations.

In practice, while Bernstein has continued to be a major figure in British sociology of education, the direct influence of Durkheim on future developments has not been as great as Karabel and Halsey anticipated. The full translation of *The Evolution of Educational Thought* was published in the same year as their collection, and a selection of newly translated writings on education was published by Pickering in 1979 within a dual-focused volume, *Essays on Morals and Education*. Both were published in hardback only, had some initial impact, but never became central to sociology of education. While occasional academic articles and book chapters drew on insights from Durkheim, it was not until the 1990s that two edited collections of articles were published which drew together and assessed Durkheim's past and present relevance to the sociology of education (Cardi and Plantier 1993, Walford and Pickering 1998).

Why should this neglect be worthy of mention? Durkheim is, after all, known as a sociologist. The previous substantial collections of articles on his work edited by Hamilton (1990 and 1995) completely ignored any contribution that Durkheim may have made to education, and few sociologists seem to have noticed this lacuna. Yet, such an omission is actually unjustifiable. Durkheim cared passionately about education, and all of his professional life was spent in direct contact with teacher education. The centrality of his belief in the importance of education is such that during the 1930s one Marxist commentator argued that:

> ... in reality everything occurred as though the founder of French sociology had written *The Division of Labour* in order to permit obscure administrators to draw up an education destined for schoolteachers. The introduction of Sociology into the Écoles Normales consecrated the administrative victory of this official morality. These were the years when Durkheim was engaged in building up his work and propagating his teaching, with great obstinacy and great authoritarian rigour, while giving that work the venerable appearance of science. In the name of that appear-

ance, in the name of science, teachers taught children to respect the French nation, to justify class collaboration, to accept everything, to join in the cult of the Flag and the bourgeois Democracy.

(P. Nizan 1932, quoted in Lukes 1973:357)

Whilst such a view is extreme, there is no doubt that the assessment of all of Durkheim's work needs to take account of the direct educational context within which he worked. It might be argued that Durkheim's contribution to the development of sociology only occurred because of his passion for education in the broadest sense, such that his educational writings should be central to an understanding of his sociology.

Durkheim was born at a time when public education was seen to be of the utmost importance to the well-being of the French nation. In spite of radical Napoleonic reforms in education, the disastrous war of 1870 was held by some to be due to a failure of an entrenched educational system which, amongst other things, was not focused sharply enough on the sciences. In France, the training of teachers in primary and secondary schools was taken much more seriously from the beginning of the nineteenth century and was much more institutionalized than it was, for example, in Britain. For those wishing to enter teaching at the secondary level, in lycées or universities, study at an Ecole Normale Supérieure was required. The best candidates often went from teaching in a lycée to lecturing in a university. Students unable to pass the exams necessary to enter the Ecole Normale Supérieure usually went straight into a university. The courses at the Ecole Normale Supérieure in Paris were of an academic standard usually held to be higher than that of the university itself. A person who successfully completed the course would have received something equivalent to an honours degree as well as a qualification in pedagogy.

Another reason that made the training of teachers so important in the eyes of the French government in Durkheim's day was the policy that the ideals of the state should be implemented by teachers themselves. The teacher was seen as the moral leader, not only in towns but in the thousands of villages of rural France. The policy of the Third Republic was to replace a rigid ecclesiastical morality with a secular one. To this end all primary schooling was made free and compulsory in 1881.

Durkheim entered the Ecole Normale Supérieure in 1879 and received his *agrégation* in 1882. He taught at three lycées for short periods and then went to lecture at the University of Bordeaux in 1887. All his university posts involved the subject of education. When he first went to Bordeaux he was appointed lecturer in social sciences and pedagogy. He gave weekly lectures on educational theory to primary school teachers, as well as lectures on sociology. Later he became professor of social science. In 1902 he became a lecturer in the science of education at the Sorbonne and gave compulsory courses in education at the Ecole Normale. He was made professor of education in 1906 but in 1913 the title was changed to include sociology. Through these prestigious positions he was able to have a fundamental influence on education. This was due to the highly centralized nature of French education which was controlled by the civil service based in Paris, and much influenced by the government in power. Thus education was always prominent in his appointments and might be said to have been his life's work, irrespective of the many books and articles he wrote on sociological subjects in general. It is estimated that three-quarters of his teaching time was given to pedagogy.

One can only speculate as to why Durkheim published so little of his work on education during his lifetime. Perhaps the very centrality of it to his life meant that he was constantly revising it and was never completely satisfied with the result. As it was, he only sent a few articles and reviews on educational subjects to be published, and the bulk of his work in this area was published posthumously. Three important books appeared, based upon his own and other people's notes from lectures courses – *Education and Sociology* (1922a), *Moral Education* (1925a), and *The Evolution of Educational Thought* (1938a). As Pickering indicates, the lectures on which these books are based were formulated around the turn of the century, which was the period during which Durkheim was at his most creative (Introduction in Pickering 1979). *Moral Education*, for example, was his most systematic treatment of teaching in schools and was given in various forms from 1889 to 1912 in Bordeaux and Paris. *The Evolution of Educational Thought* was similarly based on a series of twenty-seven lectures which started life in Paris and continued for many years. The opening lecture from this course was, in fact, published in 1906 and was included in the set of four essays edited by Fauconnet published under the title of *Education and Sociology*. None of these three was translated into English until after the Second World War – much later than the other major works by Durkheim – a further indication of the way his educational work was ignored.

However, while Durkheim's influence on the sociology of education might not be as great as he deserved, there have still been numerous significant articles, and there was something of a resurgence of interest in the late 1990s. The articles referred to here as Selected Items illustrate the diversity of ways in which current sociologists of education (and, indeed, some who might regard themselves as philosophers of education) have drawn on Durkheim's work. They illustrate different types of engagement with Durkheim's work on education. In some of the items selected for reprinting, Durkheim's writings are at the centre and the authors discuss his thought about various aspects of education in a detailed and critical way. In contrast, other items start by focusing on particular educational problems and issues and look to Durkheim's work for illumination and understanding. These authors present up-to-date discussion of current areas of concern and use a Durkheimian framework to structure their analysis.

The much neglected work of Durkheim, his magisterial lectures published as *The Evolution of Educational Thought* (1938a), and already alluded to, is the subject of the article by Robert Alun Jones. Durkheim was critical of the educational reforms then taking place in France because they neglected the moral basis of education – 'ideals cannot be legislated into existence' he said. Durkheim, secularist and rationalist that he was, showed a deep appreciation of the medieval Christian church, not least because of its organic aim of educating the 'whole person'.

A concept which is basic to sociology and education is socialization, the term that emphasizes a process in which a society's values and 'know how' are absorbed into an individual. Durkheim used the term in a broad way by referring to socialization as educating the young so that they become mature adults. Simply it means for him, 'humanization'. De Gaudemar, who sees that the term socialization is not without difficulties, also stresses how Durkheim derived many of his ideas on education from Christianity.

Mohamed Cherkaoui, is also concerned with *The Evolution of Educational Thought in France* and draws out parallels and differences between Durkheim's and Bernstein's theories of educational systems and highlights Bernstein's reformulation of certain features of Durkheim's thought. This is followed by a chapter by Brian Davies, which is one of the few articles within the *British Journal of Sociology of Education* to draw explicitly on Durkheim. Davies reviews Durkheim's place in the development of sociology of education in Britain. He argues that for many years Durkheim was misrepresented as a conservative anti-hero, and that the only important exception to this was the work of Bernstein.

Mark Cladis examines the nature of Durkheim's conception of moral education, along with a discussion of the extent to which that conception is appropriate for pluralistic democracies [Cladis 1998]. It shows that Durkheim's approach to education was essentially that of the historicist who understands education as a collection of practices and institutions that have been organized slowly in the course of time. His idea of public education was one that embraced moral individualism and can be seen as one of the best examples that we have of democratic education. Cladis argues that Durkheim's heteroge-neous work on moral education embraces: critical thought and shared traditions, autonomy and community, human diversity and social unity. The chapter offers a nuanced description of and challenge to liberal, democratic institutions. It champions various authoritative perspectives of society's shared under-standings, as a means to cultivate in students dispositions for life in complex, pluralistic societies.

W. S. F. Pickering focuses on Durkheim's views on the admin-istration of punishment in schools. Durkheim, in his lectures on *Moral Education* published posthumously in 1925, provides a comprehensive and closely argued case against the use of corpo-ral punishment in schools. It is based on his deep-seated humanism associated with the Third Republic and *la morale laïque* (secular morality). His argument turns on the conviction that any form of physical punishment dehumanizes the child. But just as important is the fact that the very moral values the teacher tries to instil in the child are negated by such punish-ment. Rehearsing Durkheim's argument has many virtues. It raises the issue of discipline and punishment in general, the object of punishment and how it should be administered. The grading of punishment, group punishment and frequency of punishment are also referred to. These points are relevant today when so much violence is found in schools. Britain was the last country in Europe to abolish corporal punishment in all schools, and in Britain and elsewhere there is always lurking the possibil-ity of a return to physical punishment.

Jean Elisabeth Pederson explores Durkheim's position on sex education in the context of his dispute with Doléris for a 'rational sex education'. Durkheim argued that anxiety about sex existed in every culture and, therefore, must be a real and not imaginary issue. In response, Doléris accused Durkheim of succumbing to the prejudices of his own background. This article attempts to understand Durkheim's viewpoint more fully by exploring the meanings of his actions in their historical context.

David Rigioni and Donald R. LaMagdeleine explore the contemporary education of computer professionals, and argue that Durkheim's emphasis on the moral dimensions of social reality are supported. In the computer department studied they found that an interlocking set of images, maxims and operating assumptions – a collective moral account – had been developed which framed the curriculum, courses and student evaluation.

The following three items deal with educational systems again. That by Roger Goodman investigates the nature of Japanese education in the light of Durkheim's views. First, Goodman presents a detailed account of one very popular conception of the present-day Japanese educational system. He takes ten elements of that system and shows that there are many similarities between this conception of Japanese education and the type of system that Durkheim thought to be ideal. However, this chapter argues that, in practice, the popular conception of the Japanese educational system is a myth. While the ideological underpinnings of the educational system might be seen to have strong parallels with Durkheim's ideas, the reality is very different. The chapter then describes an alternative conception of the Japanese system, which includes the widespread private sector, and shows that the system is far from the ideal type that Durkheim envisaged.

Mark Cladis argues that a public education system similar to that recommended by Durkheim is a condition for a flourishing liberal society [Cladis, 1995]. He argues that Durkheim mingled standard liberal and communitarian values – values supporting individual rights and critical thought on the one hand and values supporting the common good and tradition on the other. Durkheim forged a middle way between liberalism and communitarianism, thereby rescuing us from the forced option that is often erected – defend 'the individual' or protect 'the community'.

Finally, Geoffrey Walford considers the links between Durkheim's views on democracy and diversity and some of the recent changes in England. The last decade has seen many changes in the English educational system that have been designed to broaden choice and diversity within the state maintained sector. However, until recently, little has been done to encourage the 'supply side' of schooling. This chapter reviews the changing nature and structure of the educational system in England, concentrating on 1993 legislation that allows the establishment of faith-based and sponsored grant-maintained schools. The chapter reviews the conditions under which new schools can be established and can operate and examines the extent and nature of implementation of the legislation. The whole development is discussed in the light of Durkheim's ideas on the nature and provision of schooling and his beliefs about the role of schools in developing social solidarity.

References

Cardi, F. and Plantier, J. (eds) (1993) *Durkheim, sociologue de l'éducation*, Paris: L'Harmattan.

Durkheim, E. (1922a) *Education et sociologie*, introduction by Paul Fauconnet, Paris: Alcan.

— (t.1956a) by S. D. Fox, *Education and Sociology*, Chicago: Free Press.

— (1925a) *L'Education morale*, introduction by Paul Fauconnet, Paris: Alcan.

— (t.1961a) by E. K. Wilson and H. Schurer, *Moral Education: A Study in the Theory and Application of the Sociology of Education*, edited, with an introduction, by E. K. Wilson, New York: Free Press.

— (1938a) *L'Evolution pédagogique en France*, 2 vols, Paris: Alcan.

— (t.1977a) by P. Collins, *The Evolution of Educational Thought in France*, London and Boston: Routledge and Kegan Paul.

Halsey, A. H., Floud, J. and Anderson, C. A. (1961) (eds) *Education, Economy, and Society*, New York: Free Press.

Hamilton, P. (1990) *Emile Durkheim: Critical Assessments*, First Series, 4 vols, London: Routledge.

— (1995) *Emile Durkheim: Critical Assessments*, Second Series, 4 vols, London: Routledge.

Karabel, J. and Halsey, A. H. (eds) (1977) *Power and Ideology in Education*, New York: Oxford University Press.

Lukes, S. (1973) *Emile Durkheim. His Life and Work: A Historical and Critical Study*, London: Allen Lane. New edn 1992, London: Penguin.

Pickering, W. S. F. (ed.) (1979) *Durkheim: Essays on Morals and Education*, London: Routledge and Kegan Paul.

Walford, G. and Pickering, W. S. F. (1998) (eds) *Durkheim and Modern Education*, London: Routledge.

Selected Items

Cherkaoui, M. (1977) 'Bernstein and Durkheim: two theories of change in educational systems', *Harvard Educational Review* 47(4):556–64.

Cladis, M. S. (1995) 'Education, virtue and democracy in the work of Emile Durkheim', *Journal of Moral Education* 24(1):37–52.

Cladis, M. S. (1998) 'Emile Durkheim and moral education in a pluralistic society', in G. Walford and W. S. F. Pickering (eds), *Durkheim and Modern Education*, London: Routledge.

Davies, B. (1994) 'Durkheim and the sociology of education in Britain', *British Journal of Sociology of Education* 15(1):3–25.

De Gaudemar, P. (1993) 'Le concept de socialisation dans la sociologie de l'éducation chez Durkheim', in F. Cardi and J. Plantier (eds), *Durkheim sociologie de l'éducation*, L'Harmattan.

Goodman, R. (1998) 'Japanese education: a Durkheimian ideal type?', in G. Walford and W. S. F. Pickering (eds), *Durkheim and Modern Education*, London: Routledge.

Jones, R. A. (1990) 'Religion and realism: some reflections on Durkheim's *L'évolution pédagogique en France*', *Archives de sciences sociales des religions* 69:69–89.

Pedersen, J. E. (1998) 'Something mysterious: sex education, Victorian morality and Durkheim's comparative sociology', *Journal of the History of the Behavioral Sciences* 34(2):135–51.

Pickering, W. S. F. (1998) 'The administration of punishment in schools', in G. Walford and W. S. F. Pickering (eds), *Durkheim and Modern Education*, London: Routledge.

Rigioni, D. P. and LaMagdeleine, D. R. (1998) 'Computer majors' education as moral enterprise: a Durkheimian analysis', *Journal of Moral Education* 27(4):319–33.

Walford, G. (1998) 'Durkheim, democracy and diversity: some thoughts on recent changes in England and Wales', in G. Walford and W. S. F. Pickering (eds), *Durkheim and Modern Education*, London: Routledge.

Chapter 10

Reflections on the interpretation of Durkheim in the sociological tradition

Sue Stedman Jones

Recognition of the foundational importance of Durkheim's work for each of the areas of social life which have just been considered, has been marred by the understanding, or perhaps misunderstanding, of his general theory. Whilst the importance of Durkheim as the founder of sociology as a rigorous scientific discipline with a unique *sui generis* subject matter – society – is beyond doubt, he has, however, been subject to almost constant critical theoretical attack from the very early days in sociology. Steven Lukes has shown the confusing range of accusations made against him: materialist and idealist, positivist and metaphysician, rationalist and irrationalist, theist and mystic, fascist, liberal and a conservative (Lukes 1973). It has rightly been observed that Durkheim is well-known but not known well.

The truth of this aphorism can be seen through an analysis of Durkheim's fate in the subject which he founded: the responses to his thought have left particular marks on its interpretation. This will show that many of the views ascribed to him, if not merely at variance with, are in some instances in contradiction to his own statements. Further, it will raise questions about those theories which can be said to have 'captured' his thought – both in the sense of imposing a definitive interpretation on it and of identifying it with their own aims and interests. These have added their own peculiar mark that does not necessarily fit with the original Durkheim at all. It is the responses to his thought,

the criticisms of it and the special pleadings of persuasive interpretations which develop a picture of 'Durkheimianism'.
Through the sum total of these, Durkheim has become a kind of
straw man who is routinely attacked despite the fact that his
influence can be seen in the very movements that now oppose
him. This is particularly clear with Foucault who is presented as
the apex of critical thinking in contrast to the old conservative
positivist Durkheim. However, many of Foucault's ideas stem
from Durkheim but this tends to be concealed through Foucault's
neologisms.

Durkheim's fate in American sociology is particularly instruc-
tive since it has been the dominant culture – ironic for a French
thinker – in interpreting him. Much that is viewed as the truth
about Durkheim and his theory stems both from his identifica-
tion with what is now viewed as conservative functionalism and
by the judgements made about him by significant figures within
this movement. But Durkheim does not adequately fit with this
earlier functionalism and has rather more affinity with the
developing movements of neo-functionalism (Alexander 1998).
His functionalism when viewed within the whole of his theoretical language is neither static, uncritical or finally opposed to
questions of meaning. All depends on the meaning of representation and its role in his thought – 'social life consists entirely in
representations' (1895a:xi/34).[1] The logic of this was signifi-
cantly passed over by Parsons, Coser and Nisbet.

In the early period of the development of American sociology, say from 1890–1917, Durkheim's thought was rejected
through the individualism and voluntarism of Gehlke and
Bristol who were opposed to his realism and his objectivism
(Hinkle 1960). This critique sets up an apparent opposition
between realism and individualism on the one hand, and voluntarism and objectivism on the other, which is antithetical to the
understanding of Durkheim. From this stems a common accusation that is still widespread in the 'underbelly' of sociology, that
is, in student texts and what is routinely said about Durkheim,
particularly in pre-university courses. It is that his account of

society denies the individual and can accommodate no conception of freedom or of will. But in fact he identifies collective will and intelligence as involved in the deepest level of structure (1900c in 1975b, I:30/369).[2] Durkheim clearly states that his view of society does not deny the individual: there is no social uniformity which invalidates 'individual gradations' (ibid.:29/367). He argues that 'society can only exist in and through individuals' (1912a:356/252) and that individuals are the 'only active element of society' (1898b:43/29). Since no sociologist has insisted more on the reality of society, the important question for the understanding of his thought is how he accounts for the reality of society without denying the individual. I suggest that this centres around a particularized form of consciouness, which denotes the individual (*conscience particulière*) and is found within a general frame of reference, that is, collective representations (see Pickering 2000).

Certainly Durkheim's theoretical stance on the complex and autonomous nature of the collectivity was opposed to the deductive rationalist character of early American sociology which defined the nature of the group by individual properties. But their manner of criticizing Durkheim led to the idea of a radical opposition between voluntarism and objectivism and his insistence on the objective reality of social facts was thereby taken to be – and continues to be – a denial *per se* of will and of agency in social action. Now it is clear that Durkheim does not hold that society springs out of effortless volitions of the individual, for it is clear that for him it has a reality and persistence that far exceeds what any one person wishes or can effect by will or action. He would agree with Comte's attack on the *philosophes* who during the Revolution of 1789 criticized society from a standpoint that was not grounded in the reality of society and presupposed society could effortlessly change through the dictat of the theorist. But it does not thereby follow that he has no account of will or of its effect in social action. Indeed an account of will and the ends that it pursues is central to his account of action (1925a:43/49)[3] and of the science of morals (1893b:xxxix/xxvii). Nor does it follow that he underestimates the effects of concerted efforts on the ills of society; the term effort is significant, for this is one way in which he accounts for will and how it passes into action (1895a:29/70). Indeed he insists that the ills of society can only be overcome through 'concerted' and 'organised' efforts (1925a:71/84). There is clearly a tension between agency and structure in Durkheim's thought; his insistence on the resistance to change of social facts is not *per se* a denial of agency.

The neglect of this is aided by widespread accusations of his determinism, particularly in the early period (cf. Lacroix 1981:60). But this overlooks his argument that freedom is not an obstacle to a science of morality or any other science, for freedom and 'determinate law' can be reconciled 'since human volitions are connected to external events' (1893b/xxxvii/xxv). It is the constant neglect of his view of will and freedom of mind that contributes to such views. Uniquely amongst Durkheimian commentators Watts Miller stresses his use of will and the fact that Durkheim does have a conception of freedom (Watts Miller 1996). But it is not just in his first book that Durkheim makes use of the concept of freedom (Durkheim 1893b). In the reputedly most positivist of his texts, *The Rules*, he acknowledges 'a freedom of thought which we actually use (*jouissons*)' (1895a:71/102). I suggest that a closer look at his theoretical language shows that Durkheim does allow for the multidimensionality of the presuppositional logic, which Alexander (1982) rightly later argues the social sciences require.

Durkheim calls society a system of forces – a definition central to Foucault's later account of power. In *Les Formes élémentaires* Durkheim calls these acting forces '*forces agissantes*' (1912a:638/448). This is a complex term but its meaning cannot be identified with nineteenth-century scientism and thermodynamics (Lukes 1982:8). How could it then come firstly from 'inner experience' (1912a:521/369)? Durkheim's analogies do not dictate the only way in which a term must be understood. I suggest he builds the power of agency into the structure of society: 'active force' is identified with 'productive power' (ibid.:519/367). There is here a complicated interaction between structure and agency and between the power of action of the individual and its development through 'association' into the power of society. This is overlooked through the false antitheses implied by these early critiques and continued through ethnomethodological critiques (Walsh in Filmer *et al.* 1972). This interaction centres around the formation of wholes through action and the subsequent objectivity and reality of a system of relations and representations. It results from this slow work of consolidation of structures that it is irreducible to any particular action or wish and which cannot be undone by dictat or by individual will. So instead of an unbridgeable opposition between realism and voluntarism, there is complex interaction between objective reality and subjective input that is unique to society.

The American response to Durkheim in the second period, 1918–29, which centred on the Chicago school, continued the rejection of Durkheim's social realism because of its metaphysical and mystical nature. This ignored Durkheim's explicit rejection of both 'metaphysics' and of 'mysticism': just as he rejected 'mystical' views of the state (1950a:90), accused Comte and Spencer of imposing a 'metaphysics' of positivism (1895a:ix) and rejected 'realism' which he associated with 'substantialism' (ibid.:xii). Indeed, it was not until Alpert's study of 1939 that Durkheim's view of the nature of the reality of society as relational social realism was recognized. A conception of relational realism is central to contemporary work on the philosophy of science and its connection with Durkheim (Schmaus 1994).

But it was the next period in American sociology that has been the most influential in terms of the dominant interpretation imposed on Durkheim. Parson's interpretation of Durkheim, together with his annexation of him as a forerunner of his own views, has been the most influential in sociology and, ever since, Durkheim has been identified with Parsonian thought. Although Parsons bypassed the earlier accusations and argued positively for Durkheim, he rescued Durkheim by allying him with his own project, or more accurately, by presenting Durkheim as a failed predecessor of his own voluntarist theory of action. Thus Durkheim exemplifies 'the positivist theory of action' – a model which breaks down as he moves towards the idealism of his later system (Parsons 1937). This view has been widely accepted and we can see the continued influence of it in Jeffrey Alexander's *Theoretical Logic in Sociology* (1982), where he sees the issue of Durkheim's early work as the reconciliation of action with collective order within the tensions of voluntarism and determinism.

Parsons initiated the conception of an epistemological break between Durkheim's early and later work, between his early positivism and his later idealism. This overlooks Durkheim's rejection of positivism in his early work (1895a:ix), his rejection of idealism (1898b) and his espousal of rationalism (1895a). This conception of an epistemological break has been challenged by recent commentators who rightly stress the centrality and constant concern with collective representations throughout his oeuvre (Schmaus 1994, Pickering 2000). Mestrovic also stresses Durkheim's constant pre-occupation with representation and associated this with Schopenhauer (Mestrovic 1988).

The business of imposing an interpretation is complex. It consists in both ignoring certain theoretical positions and statements and re-defining others in terms of different issues and problematics. It was through Parsons' and Nisbet's interpretation that Durkheim became a theorist obsessed with the problem of social order. This view of Durkheim coincided with a sense of economic crisis in America (Hinkle 1960). He was thus identified and continues to be presented as a theorist who is consistently concerned with problems of order and the danger of social disorganization and social breakdown. Parsons identifies Durkheim's conception of solidarity with 'the system' and concern for its integration; in this way he presents Durkheim as primarily concerned with the integration of the social system.

This is clear in his essay 'Durkheim's contribution to the theory of the integration of social systems' (Parsons 1960), where he identifies organic solidarity with 'the functional necessity underlying institutionalisation' and 'the integration of units' within a common value system, and further, with aspects of the motivational commitment to society and 'to conformity with expectations institutionalised within it' (ibid.:121). Thus Parsons treats solidarity as though it is one and the same thing as the system and its integration.

Certainly the systematic nature of solidarity and its different social and historical forms is central to the theoretical possibility of sociology for Durkheim. But after Parsons' interpretation, Durkheim is viewed as being obsessed with the integration of the social and this is taken as definitive of his whole endeavour. However, where in the corpus of his writing does Durkheim argue for such a position? Indeed, where does Durkheim talk about the social system in the way that Parsons does, as that which is opposed to what is systematically available to observation in the actual relations of society? True, he talks about different forms of solidarity and different forms of social consciousness. Nowhere, however, does he talk of a system that so effectively transcends the relations which make up a society that these can be seen to derive from it and which require the normative stability of the system for integration to occur. And further, is he concerned with integration in the way that Parsons characterizes it? Although Parsons recognized that Durkheim is outlining a 'special type of interdependence generated by functional differentiation' he ignores Durkheim's explicit acknowledgement that differentiated economy requires autonomy and reflection on the part of the person.

Assuredly, Durkheim clearly hoped for adequate relatedness within the complex and tortured birth of modern society but he clearly did not believe that normative integration could occur without justice and equality. We can see from Book III of the *Division of Labour* that he viewed these as lacking in contemporary society. Indeed nowhere can he be said to want integration within a system at the expense of justice, equality, individuation and personal autonomy. So Parsons ignores Durkheim's riders that organic solidarity is only possible with equality (1893b:370–1). Whilst Parsons talks about integration through a common value system, he does not mention equality or conceives of it as central to the possibility of integration. By contrast, for Durkheim 'all external inequality compromises organic solidarity' (ibid.:373). But the picture Parsons paints, with no acknowledgement of the latter considerations, is part and parcel of the 'conservative' Durkheim, who is obsessed with order and integration at all costs. This false idea remains so widespread in sociology.

So, by sleight of hand and neglect of crucial statements, Parsons adheres solidarity to the 'system' and its functional integration. And here is the way Durkheim has been viewed, not just among students through introductory texts, but by their teachers in sociology for whom Parsons has been the crucial and definitive commentator on Durkheim. In Durkheim there is no Parsonian conception of the functional prerequisites of a system or a concern with latency, equilibrium, the problem of social control, and the study of actors in terms of deviance and conformity. Yet Parsons associates these terms with Durkheim (Parsons 1937:376). Is Durkheim's view of constraint and sanction central to social control? This is to presuppose the meaning of sanction and to gloss over the distinction between legitimate and illegitimate constraint. But this is to take him out of context both culturally and politically and above all to ignore the use of solidarity by French socialists. Certainly there are different uses of the term solidarity and some defined by right-wing thinkers in France. But the use of solidarity in combination with the search for justice and equality in social relations mark out Durkheim's socialist sympathies. So, rather than acknowledging Durkheim's view of modern society in a dynamic movement towards justice, his central problematic is seen as 'what holds societies together'. Fortunately, later sociologists recognize that Durkheim aims at transformation towards new orders (Joas 1993). They understand his fundamental democratic impulse (Müller 1993) and show the similarities with Marx (Pearce 1989).

It was during this third period in American sociology that a recognition of his science of morals began; but once more it was annexed to a conservative vision of social control. But this overlooked the significance of the science of morals in a historical context. In terms of French philosophy and politics this was far from conservative, as has been recognized recently by Turner (1992). Certainly, 'the work of justice' for Durkheim is central to the tasks facing modern society. It is part of his criticism of the established order in the closing pages of *The Division of Labour* and it was the goal of contemporary Jaurèsian socialism. The logic of justice forms part of Renouvier's influential *Science de la Morale* (1869). To be sure, the conservative thinkers, through whom Nisbet interprets Durkheim, would not have opposed justice for the established social order, which represented God's will in the eyes of such conservatives. Saint-Simon, who introduced the idea of science of morals into French thought, was the founder of French socialism. The great interest and importance of Durkheim's science of ethics and its centrality to a dynamic and critical view of society has been demonstrated by Watts Miller's *Durkheim, Morals and Modernity* (1996). With a work of such originality and scholarship a whole new vision of Durkheim's ethical project has been initiated.

Durkheim's project of a science of morals was viewed as conservative in theoretical terms for it was taken to imply that science and its facts must be the basis of values. Durkheim (1924a) denies this and says neither the facts of biology, psychology or sociology are its basis and argues for the autonomy of the science of morals (1893b:xxxvii/xxv). This was further taken to entail the derivation of the ought from the is – value from fact. Thus the logic of his conservatism was fixed, since this was taken as meaning value = fact = existing order. Durkheim as the theorist of the *status quo* and order was again reinforced.

Now if this were true then Durkheim would not only be condemned morally to the *status quo*, he would also be incapable of conceiving of a dynamic morality that moves beyond present inadequacies. He would also have committed that famous philosophical error – the naturalistic fallacy of trying to derive an ought from an is. But this interpretation overlooks the question of how reality is accessed, that is, how we grasp a fact. It also neglects the logic of critique of this. He raises both issues in 'Jugements de valeur et jugements de réalité' (Durkheim 1911b), where it is clear that the logic of judgement is central to the definition of any reality for Durkheim and that through this he rejects a fact-value separation. 'There is not one way of thinking and of judging to establish the existent and another for evaluation' (ibid.:119/95). For him there is only one faculty of judgement which is the basis of both fact and value. All judgement employs ideals but there are different types of ideals. The ideals involved in judgements that are concerned with the expression of reality are 'properly speaking concepts' (ibid.:120/95). Here the ideal serves as symbol for the thing to render it available to thought. However, ideals of value are concerned 'with transfiguring the reality to which they are connected' (ibid.). Thus the ideal as central to judgement has a transformative potential and this, Durkheim claims, rescues 'positive sociology' from the 'empiricist fetishism' of which it is often accused (ibid.:120/96). Although this is a late essay the logic of the ideal as a dynamic of transformation is also present in his early work (1893b:331/279).

Durkheim's distinction of the normal and the pathological was similarly seen as central to his conservatism. The equation of the abnormal with disorganization and disorder was fixed and conversely normal was seen as equivalent to 'order' and the *status quo*. Again, a closer analysis of Durkheim's texts should have revealed a far more complicated picture. In fact it is the obverse of this dismal view, which nevertheless continues down the years. Giddens has argued rightly that the normal was not equivalent to the *status quo* (1971), which is clear in Durkheim's argument that 'abnormal' social constraint is that based on power or wealth and particularly when wealth does not express 'social value' (1895b:122n1/146n23). Similarly, anomie has been tied to the flag of conservative normalization and is subsequently seen as indicating anything unusual, unregulated or delinquent. Besnard (1987) points to the difference between Durkheim's use of anomie which was critical and non-conservative and the later uses of the term which obscure this.

The view of Durkheim's conservatism was reinforced by more recent commentators in American sociology – Nisbet and Coser. Nisbet's interpretation has been the most influential in student texts, where they continue to represent Durkheim as an organicist positivist who is concerned with order (Bilton 1981). Despite the opposition of his view by Giddens (1971), La Capra (1972) and Lukes (1973), and by some dark law which governs the interpretation of Durkheim, the worst and least historically accurate interpretation seems to triumph. Nisbet held that positivism and conservatism were the intellectual sources of Durkheim's thought (Nisbet 1965:24). This association of positivism and conservatism (stressed not only by Nisbet but accepted by Coser and Gouldner) neglects not only the development of a left-positivism under the Third Republic but also Durkheim's explicit espousal of rationalism as the philosophical marker for his brand of theory (1895a:ix/33).

For Nisbet, the post-revolutionary thinkers de Maistre and de Bonald are the philosophical sources of Durkheim's conservatism (Nisbet 1952:16; and see Nisbet 1966). His central argument for this position centres around Durkheim's conception of the primacy of society, which was stressed by the post-revolutionary conservatives against Enlightenment individualism. Through this proposition Nisbet also imposed a conservatism on Durkheim's interest in authority and in religion. Of course Nisbet offers no good reason why the republican Durkheim should have turned to these thinkers as sources of his thought. This infamous and unjustified assertion takes Durkheim quite out of political context and ignores the struggles of the Republicans in the early years of the Third Republic against the traditionalism inspired by precisely these thinkers who opposed the very idea of a republic. They wanted the return of the monarchy and with it the order and hierarchy sustained by the Church. Thus these post-revolutionary thinkers opposed Cartesian rationalism and the method of doubt, free thought, individualism and the concept of personal autonomy – all of which were espoused by Durkheim (see 1893b:xlii/xxix;1897a:430/375). They admired medievalism with its order, hierarchy and the dominance of the Church; on the contrary Durkheim believed that sociology could only be developed through abandoning traditionalism and espousing what the traditionalists condemned – the power of reason (1915a/1964:383). It is no wonder after Nisbet's interpretation that Durkheim is regarded as a thinker who wanted order and hierarchy – a view which is still being promulgated in students' texts (Bilton 1981). But just as there is no evidence that he was obsessed with integration at all costs, there is no evidence that order is Durkheim's main preoccupation and no evidence that he desired a hierarchy similar to medieval society as did the true French conservatives, although he had a certain fascination for medievalism. Indeed his references to a hierarchy of values links him to a form of post Saint-Simonian socialism. Nisbet's view is incompatible with the democratic pluralism and individualism which Durkheim espoused.

Further, although Nisbet, against the earlier accusations, put a good spin on Durkheim's realism, he identified this with that of traditionalism, especially that of de Bonald. In this way Nisbet has imposed a view of Durkheim's social realism that is not only incompatible with the autonomy of reflection and of action, but which requires their denial. This has been widely accepted and has continued ever since in the 'underbelly' of sociology. But the analogy requires an identity between de Bonald's and Durkheim's view of language which does not hold. The primacy of language over reason is central to the sociologism of de Bonald. He held that language is necessary for the possibility of society. The transcendence of society over the individual (central to the logic of sociologism) is demonstrated through the divine origin of language. This apology for revelation opposes the autonomy of the person and of intellectual judgement through the divine origin of language which demonstrated its purported dominance of reason. But for Durkheim the opposite is the case. Thought is logically anterior to language: 'The affinity of ideas communicate themselves to words which represent them' (1893b:51/42). Durkheim, on the contrary, identified the necessity of free critical thought in the Cartesian method of doubt (ibid.:xlii) and in identifying the 'personal ideal' with 'autonomy of action' (1912a:605/425).

The reality of society, for Durkheim, centres on the reality of relations and the relational structures that surround us. Our dependence on solidarity cannot be presented as the equivalent of de Bonald's conception of social realism which requires the necessity for hierarchy and social obedience and opposition to personal autonomy. Of course for Durkheim language that expresses thought (through signs), also expresses social reality. But it does not follow that there is therefore no individual reason or freedom of mind for Durkheim. He does have a sense of 'reason' (ibid.:19/13) and of freedom: even in what is usually regarded as his early positivist and determinist phase he talks of the 'free functioning of our psychic life' (1893b:65/53). Indeed without an account of these, his account of the individualism that characterizes the modern era would be theoretically weakened – 'intellectual individualism appears with the reign of scientific truth; and it is even that individualism which has made it necessary' (1955a:185).

Of course by now the stage was set for a full-scale statement of his conservatism, not only by Nisbet (1952) but also by Coser (1960). Conservatism was seen by Coser as an inclination to maintain the existing order of things and to defend an order that seemed threatened. Now if this was so, why did he stress the search for justice and equality and complain that society lacks a morality? Filloux (1977) shows that Durkheim's alleged conservatism completely overlooks his interest in the suppression of the inheritance laws and the transformation of economic and political institutions. This indicates an interest in change – his 'reforming will' is the secret dynamic of Durkheimianism (ibid.:330–1). Filloux shows that this excludes neither elements of risk nor rebellion. I suggest further that this must be read in the context of the effective failure of the revolutions in nineteenth-century France to secure lasting change and stable republics, and which tended to subsequently also provoke reaction. Durkheim's claim that his method is not revolutionary and is 'conservatory' (*conservatrice*) is the source of his 'purported conservatism' (1893b:xl/xxviii). To be 'conservatory' towards social facts, that is, towards 'ways of seeing' and 'ways of acting', is to respect their reality as highly tenacious forces in action. It is to acknowledge that they cannot be overturned at will by the theorist. To view these as collective facts in his day was neither liberal nor conservative in political terms. Indeed there is also here an element of respect for the views of the common people that was more char-acteristic of socialism than conservatism. This is confirmed by his view that any authority must respect the beliefs of the people. 'Wherever a leading power establishes itself, its first and principal function is to respect the beliefs, traditions, collective practices, that is to say to defend the common conscience against all its internal and external enemies' (ibid.:51/42).

Coser (1960) held that Durkheim wrote 'during a period of social disorganisation' and that this was the background to his conservatism. Actually the Third Republic, although disturbed by frequent changes of government and threatened by enemies on the right (ideologically supported by those famous traditionalist thinkers through whom Nisbet interprets Durkheim, as we have noted), was the only successful Republican regime in nineteenth-century France. It was viewed by socialists and democrats alike as the sole condition for political stability and real change. Moreover, it was through this that the left began to make parliamentary gains and it was especially important for Durkheim's close friend Jaurès, who became the leader of the unified socialist party. Durkheim's thought in many ways represents the republican ideal and support for democratic change. This is in contrast to radical change in the history of nineteenth-century France which had been a prelude to reactionary retaliation – something that was especially evident with Napolean III's *coup d'état* after the 1848 revolution and the short-lived Second Republic.

The views expressed by Coser and Nisbet were developed before the work of Filloux who in his *Durkheim et le socialisme* (1977) stressed the Saint-Simonian vision of socialism that is present in Durkheim's works. Subsequently, the inadequacy of the long-lived conservative image of Durkheim has been questioned by Pearce (1989), Mestrovic (1988) and by the essays in *The Radical Sociology of Durkheim and Mauss* (Gane 1992). Unfortunately we do not have the benefit of Filloux's or other works of French Durkheimian scholarship (especially Besnard's *L'Anomie* 1987) in translation. Thus, the earlier views of Nisbet and Coser have a remarkable persistence despite significant work to the contrary. It can only finally be explained through their dominance in student textbooks and through the prominence of American culture on the English-speaking world of sociology in a certain significant period.

In Gouldner's *The Coming Crisis of Western Sociology* (1970) Durkheim emerges as the chief villain for all the woes of structural functionalism. Gouldner reinforces the equation of functionalism with conservatism, which continues to this day and is part of the reason for the loss of interest of the concept of function in the social sciences. But there is no such equation for Durkheim. His functionalism is dynamic and changeful and nowhere bears the mark of the static and conservative values with which it is constantly berated. 'To remain adapted, the function must be always ready to change, to accommodate itself to new situations . . . nothing immobilises a function than to be tied to a too defined structure' (1893b:323/272–3).

Running alongside these baleful interpretations was the tendency to contrast Durkheim radically with Weber. In opposition to Durkheim, Weber is seen as offering the action approach to society, but action is central to Durkheim's definition of society! He writes: 'It is through common action that it becomes conscious (*conscience*) of and establishes itself: it is above all an active co-operation' (1912a:598/421). This opposition supports the accusation that Durkheim ignores the question of *verstehen* and the role of understanding on the part of the agent and of the theorist. In later movements of sociology, which have been inspired by phenomenological philosophy, Durkheim emerges as the author of sociological positivism and thus the thinker who demonstrates the error of neglecting questions of meaning and understanding. Thus whilst the early accusations berate him for his metaphysics, later movements accuse him of positivism and scientism! But this is to overlook his use of representation and its association with mind and mental factors (1895a:xi/34).

Phenomenology and ethnomethodology, which built on Parsons' accusation that Durkheim ignored the difference between social and natural phenomena (Parsons 1937:399), reinforce the belief that Durkheim's view of science is seen as opposed to understanding. However, Durkheim's notion of science is complicated and does result in facts and laws but he is clear that its foundation lies in the understanding. *The Rules*, viewed as the most positivistic of his texts, nevertheless contains the view that good science is the product of thinking with the understanding (1895a:34/74). In other words, understanding is at the root of the scientific viewpoint. Further, he acknowledges that, through defining social facts as 'ways of acting, thinking and feeling' (ibid.:4/51), understanding is crucial to the orientation of the agent in social reality. Nevertheless, the way he is presented is that facts and laws oppose understanding, that is, *verstehen*.

So it is held that through modelling his sociology on the natural sciences, he 'violated' hermeneutics (Meadwell

1995:189). Questions of interpretation and interpretive methods have dominated recent sociology, and this is part and parcel of a trend towards aesthetic and linguistic concerns developed in the flight from positivism and its concerns of facts, laws and causality. It is clear, however, that Durkheim does not neglect questions of interpretation, for they are part of the examination of social types (1895a:89). The interpretation of social facts as ways of thinking and acting must take place under the type of society and its constituent structures. This seems to be eminently fair and sensible and in this way he grounds all questions of interpretation in the reality and structure of the society concerned. But in insisting on the necessity for support of interpretation by causality and the claim that only this provides fully adequate explanation is to ask for what Weber also demanded – the final causal and empirical verification of interpretative explanations. But whilst Weber is praised, Durkheim is condemned for his 'positivism' in contemporary views on method!

The opposition between Weber and Durkheim – representing two distinct traditions of sociology, the subjective and meaning-orientated versus the objective and the functional – has been questioned in a recent collection of articles, *Durkheim et Weber – vers la fin des malentendus*, edited by Coenen-Hunter and Hirschorn (1994). In this collection Tiryakian shows that both thinkers stress the inter-subjective validity of society and history; the contribution of both to a theory of action is explored by Coenen-Hunter; Joas stresses the creativity of action for both thinkers; and Boudon argues for Durkheim's non-positivist theory knowledge in his theory of magic where he appeals to postulates and psychological assumptions and thus to questions of internal validity.

Lukes' introduction to the 1982 translation by W. D. Halls of *The Rules* has become infamous for its denunciation of Durkheim's errors. Lukes claims that Durkheim aims at an 'absolutist' conception of knowledge that neglects the problem of relativism and aims at a knowledge of the social independent of the meanings it has for social subjects (Lukes 1982:12). This is 'sterile' compared with the hermeneutic approach. The aims of generality, objectivity and externality are at odds with the internal and subjective character of social facts. It neglects all 'micro' issues and questions of psychology. Thus his macro-theory rests on 'unexamined and implausible foundations' (ibid.:18). And through his false ideal of scientific detachment he neglects the extra-scientific and the political context of science. He neglects the question of power understood as struggle and dependency (ibid.:22).

These accusations must be challenged: Lukes reads Durkheim through Cartesianism and thereby accuses Durkheim of absolutism. But this is to overlook Durkheim's rejection of Cartesianism as an archaic and narrow form of rationalism – 'we must not cling to it' (1900b/1973:22). He rejects its insistence on simplicity and clarity and its deductivism (1925a:252), against which he not only stresses the complex and the 'obscure' in the character of social reality, but also stresses observation in method. But most importantly he insists that 'There is a relativism of truth which is historically established' (1955a:201). Through the influence of his 'educator' Renouvier, he acknowledged the relative and *différence*, and rejected philosophical realism, which is to be understood as a reflectionist, objectivist view of reality – a 'mirror of nature' (1893b:64/1895a:ix).

These accusations ignore his logic of representation – it is in this that he deals with the micro and questions of meaning signification and action. 'For a long time we have only recognised value in an action if it is intentional, that is, if the agent represents in advance what the action consists in' (1925a:101/120). This is compounded by Lukes's insistence that representation is a post-1895 concept, yet it is clearly evident both in *Les Règles* and in *De la Division du travail social* (see Pickering 2000). Through the logical structure of representation and particularly through the conception of *conscience particulière*, which is the necessary, if not the sufficient, condition of social life, an orientation of *conscience* to a determinate aspect of reality is built into the very logical foundations of his thought. As I have suggested *particulière* indicates the individuated aspect of consciousness as opposed to its collective aspect. The neglect of the theoretical significance of *conscience* amongst his commentators, and particularly of the meaning of *particulière*, has allowed such accusations to go unchallenged. However through the concept of *conscience*, Durkheim does deal with the micro-logical aspect of human reality. As with many questions in the interpretation of Durkheim, it is the peculiarity of the scientific language in which he articulates these questions that has given rise to so many problems. There is a deep misunderstanding of his scientific language, particularly *psychique, force, chose, tendance* and so on.

Thus, it is not true that Durkheim neglected psychology. He acknowledged the importance of 'a formal psychology, which is common ground between individual psychology and sociology' (1895a:xviii). In addition, we now know this from his 1895 letter to Bouglé (14/2/1895) where he explicitly denies the view widely held that his sociology is anti-psychologistic. Indeed he says it 'is a psychology' but distinct from individual psychology (Durkheim 1976). Nor did he neglect the bonds between people and groups, which is the significance of 'association'.

Nor does he entirely neglect the concept of power. This misunderstanding is due to the insistence of Lukes and others that force gains its meanings from the analogy with thermodynamics and electricity (Lukes 1982:8). Of course it is true that Durkheim does not underscore power as dependency and struggle. His search is for the conditions for solidarity aimed at a more optimistic and practical solution to the power struggles of the modern world than that entailed by Weber's bleak vision of power and modern society. Indeed Durkheim's view of society as a system of forces long antedates Foucault's analysis of power relations as a system of forces. But he goes beyond the negativity and limitations of Foucault's account and shows how power can be positive and useful in the creation and sustaining of viable communities through the forces and efforts of agency to create and sustain solidarity structures. In addition, he gives a criterion of the distinction between legitimate and illegitimate power. The latter is 'abnormal' constraint based on wealth and power – the ineffectiveness of action engendered during periods of social malaise and the damage to the autonomy and full expressiveness of human personality.

In terms of the general epistemological understanding of his theoretical outlook, it is undoubtedly true that the word 'thing' has initiated many of the attacks made on Durkheim. It is central to Parsons' charge that Durkheim overlooks the difference between social and natural phenomena, and to that of the ethnomethodologists that through this Durkheim reduces the human to the non-human and neglects the processes whereby social reality is meaningful and an emergent property of interaction. How can the inner structures of society be treated as a 'disembodied thing'? (Walsh in Filmer 1972:38). All commentators on Durkheim assume that this indicates an alliance with positivism, although Hirst (1975) acknowledged the non-positivist character of Durkheim's science. Keat and Urry (1984:85) assume that thereby Durkheim is part positivist, part essentialist. This overlooks the fact that no consistent nineteenth-century positivist would use the word thing as such. Certainly Comte does not use the term to indicate his methodological approach to reality. For a consistent positivist all reality must be analysed into law and phenomena, which are the fundamental terms for all scientific approaches to reality.

What is important is to show how this claim is compatible with Durkheim's rejection of the positivist metaphysics of Comte and Spencer and his professed rationalism. For this reason, in my article 'What does Durkheim mean by thing?' (1996) and in 'Durkhein Reconsidered (2001), I argue first, that his puzzling claim must be compatible with the claim for the representational nature of social reality; and second, that rather than his theory being based on an inappropriate science of nature and thus founding a materialist and positivist account through his use of this term, it actually answers those issues that Durkheim is not supposed to account for – meaning and signification.

From all the criticisms and accusations thrown at him in the history of his subject, it would appear that the only reason to read Durkheim would be to profit by his mistakes. Yet somehow interest in him refuses to die. Indeed, given the current interest in representations in the social sciences, Durkheim's work can be seen to offer fundamental reflections (Pickering 2000). Certainly his concept of the autonomy of collective representations and the symbolic is central to the study of culture. Indeed, early on in the interpretation of his thought his rejection of the innate and the instinctive was recognized as crucial to the determination of the cultural sphere (Hinkle 1960:276). Mestrovic (1988) has argued for the positive value of Durkheim as a corrective to the nihilism of post-modernism. Further, Durkheim's concept of collective effervescence is seen to be increasingly important as a means of social and historical analysis (see Chapter 3). One can also point to the interest in solidarity and communicative rationality by Habermas, despite Habermas's critiques of Durkheim. In fact, he has Durkheim as a forerunner rather than as an enemy (Habermas 1981). Again, Durkheim is not so much an unreconstructed authoritarian, but someone who demonstrates the reconciliation of authority and freedom, and autonomy and solidarity. Thus, rather than being the positivist apologist for lost hierarchies, his sociology demonstrates a theoretical *actualité* and speaks to the nature of a social world that is in the process of being born.

Notes

1. In references where there are two page numbers separated by / , the first refers to the page in the French text indicated. The second refers to the page in the English translation, the details of which, as well as those of the French text, are given in the References below.

However, many of the translations actually given are by the author of this introduction. The French texts use the dating-enumeration of Lukes (see Lukes 1973).

2. The original reads: 'Ces normes impersonelles de la pensée et de l'action sont celles qui constitutent le phénomène sociologique par excellence et il existe entre elles et la société le même rapport qu'entre les fonctions vitales et l'organisme: elles dépendent de l'intelligence et la volonté collective'. The latter phrase is translated by K. Wolff as 'they tell the manner from which derive collective intelligence and will'. This translation reflects my point.

3. Note that the translation by Wilson and Schnurer of 1961 eradicates Durkheim's reference to will here.

References

Alexander, J. (1982) *Theoretical Logic in Sociology*, Berkeley: University of California Press.

Alexander, J. (1998) *Neo-functionalism and After*, Oxford: Blackwell.

Alpert, H. (1939) *Emile Durkheim and his Sociology*, New York: Columbia University Press.

Besnard, P. (1987) *L'Anomie*, Paris: Presses Universitaires de France.

Bilton, T. *et al.* (1981) *Introductory Sociology*, London: Macmillan.

Coenen-Huther, J. and Hirschorn, M. (1994) *Durkheim, Weber vers la fin des malentendus*, Paris: Editions Harmattan.

Coser, L. (1960) 'Durkheim's conservatism and its implications for his sociological theory', in K. H. Wolff (ed.) *Emile Durkheim, 1858–1917*, Columbus: Ohio State University Press.

Durkheim, E. (1893b) *De la Division du travail social*, Paris: Alcan.

— (1986) 11th edn, Quadrige/Presses Universitaires de France.

— (t.1984) by W. D. Halls, *The Division of Labour in Society*, London: Macmillan.

— (1895a) *Les Règles de la méthode sociologique*, Paris: Alcan.

— (1987) 23rd edn, Quadrige/Presses Universitaires de France.

— (t.1982) by W. D. Halls, *The Rules of Sociological Method*, London: Macmillan.

— (1897a) *Le Suicide: étude de sociologie*, Paris: Alcan.

— (1986) 10th printing, Quadrige/Presses Universitaires de France.

— (t.1951) by J. A. Spaulding and G. Simpson, *Suicide: a study in sociology*, London: Routledge and Kegan Paul.

— (1898b) 'Représentations individuelles et représentations collectives', *Revue de métaphysique et de morale* 6:273–302. Reproduced in 1924a.

— (1900b) 'La Sociologie en France au XIXe siècle', *Revue bleue*, 4e série, 12:609–13, 647–52. Repr. 1987 in J.-C. Filloux (ed.) *La Science sociale et l'action*, Presses Universitaires de France.

— (t.1973) by M. Traugott in R. N. Bellah (eds) *Emile Durkheim on Morality and Society: selected writings*, Chicago: University of Chicago Press.

— (1900c) 'La sociologia ed il suo domininio scientifico', *Rivista italiana di Sociologia* 4:127–48. Repr. 1975b.

— (t.1960) K. H. Wolff (ed.) *Emile Durkheim, 1858–1917*, Columbus: Ohio State University Press.

— (1911b) 'Jugements de valeur et jugements de réalité' in 1924a.

— (1912a) *Les Formes élémentaires de la vie religieuse*, Paris: Alcan.

— (t.1995) by K. Fields, *The Elementary Forms of Religious Life*, New York: The Free Press.

— (1915a) 'La Sociologie', in *La Science française*, Paris: Ministère de l'Instruction Publique et des Beaux-Arts, I:39–49. 1960 English translation, see 1900c.

— (1924a) *Sociologie et philosophie*, Paris: Alcan.

— (t.1953) D. F. Pocock, London: Cohen & West.

— (1925a) *L'Education morale*, Paris: Alcan.

— (t.1961) E. K. Wilson and H. Schnurer, *Moral Education*, New York: Free Press.

— (1950a) *Leçons de sociologie: physique des moeurs*, University of Istanbul. Publications of the Faculty of Law no. 111, Presses Universitaires de France.

— (1990) Repr. Quadrige/Presses Universitaires de France.

— (t.1957) by C. Brookfield, *Professional Ethics and Civic Morals*, London: Routledge.

— (1992) new edition with an introduction by B. S. Turner.

— (1955a) *Pragmatisme et sociologie*, Paris: Vrin.

— (1975b) *Durkheim, E: Textes*, 3 vols, edited with an introduction by V. Karady, Paris: Les Editions de Minuit.

— (1976) 'A propos de Durkheim. Lettres à Celestin Bouglé', *Revue Française de Sociologie* 17:165–80.

Filloux, J.-C. (1977) *Durkheim et le socialisme*, Geneva: Librairie Droz.

Filmer, P. *et al.* (1972) *New Directions in Sociological Theory*, London: Collier-Macmillan.

Gane, M. (ed.) (1992) *The Radical Sociology of Durkheim and Mauss*, London: Routledge.

Giddens, A. (1971) *Capitalism and Modern Social Theory*, 1974 edn, Cambridge: Cambridge University Press.

Gouldner, A. (1970) *The Coming Crisis of Western Sociology*, London: Heinemann.

Habermas, J. (1981) *The Theory of Communicative Action*, 1991 edn, Oxford: Polity Press.

Hinkle, R. C. (1960) 'Durkheim in American Sociology', in K. H. Wolff (ed.) *Emile Durkheim, 1858–1917*, Columbus: Ohio State University Press.

Hirst, P. Q. (1975) *Durkheim, Bernard and Epistemology*, London: Routledge and Kegan Paul.

Joas, H. (1993) 'Durkheim's intellectual development', in S. Turner (ed.) *Emile Durkheim: Sociologist and Moralist*, London: Routledge.

Keat, R. and Urry, J. (1984) *Social Theory as Science*, London: Routledge and Kegan Paul.

La Capra, D. (1972) *Emile Durkheim: Sociologist and Philosopher*, Chicago: University of Chicago Press.

Lacroix, B. (1981) *Durkheim et la politique*, Montréal: Presses de l'Université de Montréal.

Lukes, S. (1973) *Emile Durkheim: His Life and Work: a historical and critical study*, London: Allen Lane.

Lukes, S. (1982) 'Introduction' to *The Rules of Sociological Method*, trans. by W. D. Halls, London: Macmillan. (See Durkheim 1895a above.)

Meadwell, H. (1995) 'Post Marxism, no friend of civil society', in J. A. Hall (ed.), *Civil Society*, Oxford: Polity Press.

Mestrovic, S. G. (1988) *Emile Durkheim and the Reformation of Sociology*, Totawa, NJ: Rowan & Littlefield.

Müller, H. P. (1993) 'Durkheim's political sociology', in S. Turner (ed.), *Emile Durkheim: Sociologist and Moralist*, London: Routledge.

Nisbet, R. (1952) 'Conservatism and sociology', *American Journal of Sociology* XVIII: 167–75.

Nisbet, R. (1965) *Emile Durkheim*, New Jersey: Prentice Hall.

Nisbet, R. (1966) *The Sociological Tradition*, London: Heinemann.

Parsons, T. (1937) *The Structure of Social Action*, New York: McGraw-Hill.

Parsons, T. (1960) 'Durkheim's contribution to the theory of the integration of social systems', in K. H. Wolff (ed.), *Emile Durkheim, 1858–1917*, Columbus: Ohio State University Press.

Pearce, F. (1989) *The Radical Durkheim*, London: Unwin Hyman.

Pickering, W. S. F. (ed.) (2000) *Durkheim and Representations*, London: Routledge.

Renouvier, C. (1869) *Science de la morale*, 2 Vols, Paris: Librairie Philosophie de Ladrange.

Schmaus, W. (1994) *Durkheim's Philosophy of Science and the Sociology of Knowledge: creating an intellectual niche*, Chicago: University of Chicago Press.

Stedman Jones, S. (1996) 'What does Durkheim mean by "thing"?', *Durkheimian Studies* 2:43–59.

Stedman Jones, S. (2001) *Durkheim Reconsidered*, Cambridge: Polity Press.

Turner, B. S. (1992) 'Preface' to 2nd edn of Durkheim's *Professional Ethics and Civic Morals*, London: Routledge. (See Durkheim 1950a.)

Watts Miller, W. (1996) *Durkheim, Morals and Modernity*, London: University College Press.

Index